Coming Out of Darkness

I0137150

Coming Out of Darkness

By Tracey L. Pagana

Copyright © 2021 Tracey L. Pagana
All rights reserved.
ISBN 9780578840246-

Dedication

    This Book is dedicated to every single person who has the courage to find a way out of the maze of darkness they find themselves encapsulated in. We, together, as a force, construct a thread of white light connection, we can and we will find safe refuge in the eye of the storm.

Thank you

Firstly, I would like to thank my spiritual director and creator of my whole entire essence and tri connection (body, mind, soul) that teaches me above all else my capacity to love fearlessly and forgive mercifully. I always feel sources power stemming from the love where source finds me, coincides with me, collaborates with me, experiences with me and continues to teach me, the subject of soul existence combining human existence forming the balance it takes to have both.

There are always so very many to thank and if I leave anyone out please know you are always alive supporting our journey as one in the middle of my heart space. For we would be nothing in this quest of spiritual teambuilding if not supported and strengthened by each other.

Team is what it means to work from your heart. Thank you to my team for the long hours of conversation, musing, brainstorming, sharing, and growing in spirit.

Thank you Laurie Smydo, Susan Talbot, Dana Jenkins and Maria Webb, for all the hours of dedication and time they spent building the message to send out to the masses. It took time and effort to sacrifice so much of your personal time and energy.

Thank you to all the brave light workers who shared a piece of themselves between the pages, all the light workers who also shared their own calling and unique tools that aid the darkness bringing light and hope to all who are seeking it.

Thank you Laurie Smydo of www.lasartstudio.com for the amazing art that graces the cover of this book channeled through your talented medium skills.

Thank Joe for always supporting me, advising me, and respecting the work that goes on in these pages that threads into our own life together.

Thank you to anyone who has grown in a session of healing, allowing the pain teaching them a place of passion and compassion allowing the hurt to heal and growth to multiply within their own sacred space. This takes more courage than anyone can know as it awakens knowledge, as well as responsibility forming a deep healing. This takes time to sit it out and allow the layers to peel away so new growth can happen.

Thank you all for having the calling that nudges you to read between the pages and the lines of this book helping you discover your own unique destiny, shedding off your own darkness, forming new boundaries of freedom and light. There is no more room for darkness that invades you when you find the light and allow the light to guide you into your own   peaceful free state of truth and existence.

v

Keep your internal torch lit, you never know when someone seeking refuge from a storm finds you because of your light. You may be the next one leading someone out of darkness, helping them find comfort within the eye of the storm. Thank you in advance for your bravery and compassionate actions.

Letter from the Editor

When Tracey asked me to edit her book, I knew it was going to be a very interesting project. I have experienced Tracey's messages from spirit both in person and in written form, whether it be in a healing session or via a text message of support. Of course Tracey wrote the book, but a lot of the chapters are actually written while Tracey was in a trance communicating with spirit. If you read the first draft of the book, it is very easy to see where Tracey was writing from her own personal experience versus the messages from Spirit. Spirit does not communicate linguistically like we humans do in written word. They are literally all over the place. They like to ramble on in run on sentences, sentences with words out of order and different tones. Tracey does not write like that, so editing each chapter was a unique experience. My hope is that I have done the best job possible translating the messages Tracey downloaded to share with the world! I can't thank Tracey enough for allowing me to participate in this process. I promise you there are so many beautiful stories, heart breaking messages and messages from spirit that will lead you on your own personal journey into the light when coming out of darkness.

Laurie Smydo, Editor

Table of Contents

Contents

Foreword

THE MOST BEAUTIFUL PEOPLE ARE THOSE WHO HAVE KNOWN DEFEAT, KNOWN SUFFERING, KNOWN STRUGGLE, KNOWN LOSS, AND HAVE FOUND THEIR WAY OUT OF THE DEPTHS. THESE PERSONS HAVE AN APPRECIATION, A SENSITIVITY, AND AN UNDERSTANDING OF LIFE THAT FILLS THEM WITH COMPASSION, GENTLENESS, AND A DEEP LOVING CONCERN. **BEAUTIFUL PEOPLE DO NOT JUST HAPPEN.**

ELISABTH KUBLER-ROSS

Tracey is one of the most beautiful people I have ever met. She has been through tremendous struggle, suffered the consequences of her choices and endured various excruciating circumstances in her life. Tracey is so beautiful to me, because she fearlessly embraces her perceived 'darkness' with compassion, forgiveness and an unwavering commitment to heal her heart and soul. She has a steadfast commitment to God and the work necessary to transform her pain and that of her clients into growth, wisdom and gratitude. I have witnessed this time and again since we started working together and then became the dearest of friends.

I met Tracey in San Francisco in spring of 2019. I had heard that her work was deeply transformative and her healing touch could heal where Western medicine fell short. While I was aware that Tracey's work could benefit me, I was, at that time, acutely focused on helping my father.

My father is a retired doctor. He and I have always had a very special connection. We especially connect over psycho-spiritual healing and a strong belief that it is a powerful compliment to Western medicine. My father has often been compared to Patch Adams, knowing that our emotional and physical health are acutely intertwined. He shared these beliefs with me since I was a child and also with his patients as far back as the 1980's, before these topics were popular.

My father took me to my first meditation course in 1989. I will never forget the miracle that occurred after our 8 week course. We had committed to meditating for one hour a day for the 8 weeks (that is a lot by anyone's standards...especially back then!). At the end of our course, my father decided to reassess his prescriptions for some chronic issues, such as high cholesterol and high blood pressure. The miracle was when his doctor informed him his labs had radically improved and the only new thing in his life was his commitment to mediation (which for him is a form of prayer). Based on his improved labs, he could eliminate or reduce various daily medications. He was thrilled, as this was a scientific example of the power of prayer/meditation. He was able to remain off of these drugs for years to come with a simple 15 minute daily mediation routine. It is now widely known that mediation reduces stress and inflammation in the body. For him, it was proof to continue to trust his intuition and to trust the support he felt compelled to offer his patients. For me, it was all I needed to commit to my own daily meditation practice and never stop.

At the time I planned to take my dad to see Tracey, he was suffering from chronic sciatica. It was debilitating for him and medicine was just not working. I traveled from my home in Mexico City to the Bay Area to collect my father and take him to our scheduled appointment. I gifted myself a session with her as well. My experience with Tracey that day was not like fireworks, instead like laying in the sunshine of my own private paradise. I felt immediately understood and so safe in her presence. I was not aware that I had so much gold to mine deep down and hidden under my peaceful veneer. I mean that in the most respectful way. Tracey sees what needs to be healed as if she is literally discovering hidden jewels! My experience with her that day was a game changer for my own healing trajectory. My father had the same experience and walked away that day pain free for the first time in years.

When Tracey opens her heart to her clients in session, she does so with God and the Angels by her side. The feeling is profound. I felt exposed yet unconditionally loved at the same time. The experience for me was one of being seen with complete acceptance, so that the shameful experiences I had kept perfectly tucked away, disguised and camouflaged, so they would remain unperceivable to even myself, were lovingly invited to slowly come out of hiding. Little did I know what a massive gift it is to share and let go of my stories. It took courage, trust and patience on my part. I decided to make a longer commitment and continue our work together. I can say that my work with Tracey is one of the best investment I have ever made! It did not take long to begin to let the light enter, heal and transmute the darkness I harbored inside. Sharing the shame, walking through the mud, being willing to 'Feel to Heal' removes the triggers in our heart and releases the negative scripting that I had been manipulated with time and again. I have come to a new place of peace and plan to never leave!

As you read the book in your hands, you will soon understand her process and also come to see that Tracey is one of the most courageous people in the world. It took great courage to put this deeply personal memoir out into the world. The call from Spirit was to write about the darkness that we all find ourselves in and the fear that accompanies it. Tracey knew that this vulnerable exposure of her own shame-filled stories, as well as the stories that were written here directly from Spirit, would provide a necessary nudge to inspire others to do the same.

It takes tremendous courage to share our stories, especially when our stories are filled with pain and what we perceive to be dark or awful. The shame we carry in our hearts is quite capable of keeping our stories and our trauma hidden for a lifetime. This is the very reason this book is so important. When we keep our stories hidden, our stories control us. They are at the core of our triggered responses, our unhealthy habits and the anxiety of our uneasy heart. The purpose of this book is to encourage you to embrace your darkness, to face your fears and form new boundaries to ensure that you can lead a life whose very foundation is based on freedom and light.

Covid has opened our eyes to the fact that nearly everyone is suffering in one form or another. No longer is depression and anxiety touching just a few, it is touching nearly everyone to different degrees. We also have many suffering from loneliness. Loneliness from actual isolation or loneliness while surrounded by others, but not living authentically. Many live as chameleons, people pleasers or empaths who chooses to care first for others, all the while negating their soul's cry to be heard, to speak without being judged, because they are afraid of what could arise. This creates tremendous loneliness and a feeling of isolation whether you are actually alone or not. I believe it is time to pull back the curtains and allow these issues to come out of hiding and to be heard with loving compassion.

It takes courage to heal. It takes courage to feel, but once on the other side, I believe you would never change the process (however uncomfortable it appears) for the deep peace and new-found joy and freedom that come from a newly healed heart and soul! This is part of the process of accessing your true beauty. As the quote says, 'Beautiful people do not just happen'. The world needs our courage and compassion now more than ever. The world needs us to step into our beauty, offering that beauty first to ourselves and then to those around us. This is where the healing lies. As they say before takeoff, 'You must first put your oxygen mask on before you can assist another!'

Tracey calls this 'living in the eye of the storm'. What she means by this, is that you can learn to live in peace no matter what is going on in your life. At the core of her guidance is learning to live in curiosity instead of judgement. 'Love them where they are at' is one of her rules of the road. Judgement cuts off our potential for a spiritual connection of any kind. How incredible would it be to feel genuine curiosity about another's very different point of view or values? If we are curious, instead of guarded or judgmental, we just might learn something new? How powerful could it be to apply that same curiosity and compassion to ourselves? To that part of ourselves that feels and thinks to differently to what we consider acceptable? How would it feel to have peaceful compassion instead feeling ashamed, angry or anxious?

Learning to live in the 'eye of the storm' is critical for us to learn to live peacefully in today's divided world. It essential for us to apply this same skill to ourselves. Imagine holding compassion for the part of you that you do not like, for the part of you that provokes great shame or embarrassment? What if we instead were genuinely curious of how it all started and why this hidden darkness has wreaked havoc in our life?

All it takes is the light of one candle to diminish darkness. It is a lot easier to do this with the help of others. Tracey helped me light this candle in our first session. I had lit thousands of candles before in my life and yet I still managed to leave certain doors in my heart bolted shut. I thought I could simply bypass them without ever knocking and still become enlightened in the way I desired. Not true. I know this now. Somehow the way in which Tracey lit the candle for me was different. Perhaps it was the entourage of the angels and guides that accompany her? Perhaps it was the gift of knowing my loved ones who had passed before me were present? Perhaps...perhaps? All I can say is that our work together was filled with light and she has gifted me with the tools so that my own candle remains lit on its own. Tracey offers individual sessions and as I mentioned above, my work with her has been the one of the single most powerful investments I have ever made!

Thank you Tracey for sharing your soul. Thank you for your guidance. Thank you for rising to the occasion by writing this powerful book. Thank you for your willingness to say 'YES" to raise your hand and tell your story. Thank you for inspiring so many others to do the same! May the walls of shame and isolation begin to disintegrate and the foundation of love and light to be born and never look back!

All my love,
Dana Jenkins

Introduction

Coming out of Darkness

I guess with a title like this, on a day like this, it should be no surprise to me that heavy freezing rain is falling from the sky in abundance. This quest to go deeper with you will take a lot of courage to talk about what needs to be discovered, exposed, and challenged as we explore what darkness really means. In truth, I have been actively avoiding the subject matter of this book: all the insecurities I harbour, tucked away, buried within myself. I knew when the message was given to me to write this book that the finished manuscript would be the most intensely passionate of all my writing. I knew deeply that I would have to hand my entirety over to Divine Source, who, in infinite wisdom, would reveal layers of hidden truth. I was planning on starting this project in Mexico, in a small town tucked up in the mountains. I had every intention to bury my entire being into this project once I arrived at my mountain destination; however, I have been hearing my soul calling me well before my trip began to start writing what was causing bubbles of toxins to release deep within my core.

The title of this book came to me in the form of a message I received in early March 2019 as I was preparing for a Body Mind and Spirit Expo in Kalamazoo, Michigan. The Expo was the weekend of March 9th and 10th. I was scheduled to speak on the Saturday afternoon. Just before my lecture was to begin, I was approached by the dedicated timekeeper of the Expo, a no- nonsense, Spirit-filled woman by the name of Beth. She walked up to me with a serious face stating "I have a message for you. I will get things set up for the next presentation and then I will come to your booth and tell you."

I went back to my booth and began seeing clients. Sometime within the next hour, Beth came to my booth. She looked me right in the eye and said, "Tracey, I only ever get messages for John (her brother-in-law) and my sister, Beverly, so this message I received for you surprised me. If I do not give it to you, it will not leave me alone. The message is: you are to write a third book and it is to be titled **Coming Out of Darkness."** She hugged me and was gone!

I was perplexed. I am not going to lie, writing a book is a huge undertaking. It requires dedication and overcoming obstacles. It is also a huge financial undertaking. It can take months of editing and rewriting, planning, and saving. It takes finding people who want to share the vision with you. In my case, artists for the covers, brave people to write the foreword, and committed people who agree to share their own experiences of healing as we continue to share with the world the tools that help discover who we are and who we are yet to become. All of this requires personal sacrifice.

I should share with you that at this point my second book was not even in the print stage when I received this message. This fact added to the anxiety around the third book rolling around in my heart chakra. I would also like to come clean and say to all of you who may be reading this, in truth, I only ever felt the need to write my first book. That need came from a place deep inside me, and that book was written at a turning point in my Spiritual life. On the other side of that coming out, I am in a stronger, more committed place.

It has been a journey of no looking back; a journey of movement and deep reflection. I invite you to journey with me in this book through the last 33 years of my life, addressing all sorts of personal growth and exploration. I found self-discovery in the experience of living every day, every moment, in awareness. This awareness, which is deeply seated in my discovering truth, helped me construct a wall of internal strength, embracing all the dark lessons that were mine to receive, uncover, and release.

So, as perplexing as it was to be called to write this message, I promised to never say no to Source. This was not leaving me any other option but to put down on paper what Spirit was calling me to share. My life partner, Joe, often commits his personal time, sharing me as he witnesses time and time again the calling Spirit puts in my path to love people. I am blessed to have a man in my life who never questions the deep calling and connection to which I said yes. I am aware Joe never truly wants me to discuss how I am connected to Spirit and what he bears witness to; how Spirit works with me; how I know, hear, and feel the need of all human life and their deep need to be loved. Joe provides safe-haven in his warm embrace, the strength of his hand in mine, the calming smile on his beautiful, peace-filled face.

Part One

Saliendo de la Oscuridad

MOCK TRIAL

When I was called to write this book in March 2019, I heard the message with my ears, but it did not totally soak into my heart until January 2020. I have been sharing the story of the message I received for months now with friends, family, and clients, trying to gather the courage to write this book. My first two books took a huge leap of faith, but this book had me feeling nervous and my stomach doing flips. I knew in my heart I was going to have to be in a place of solitude and loneliness so that I might hear the messages and share my experiences.

I started thinking in my head "how is this time to write this book supposed to present itself?" Then, as always, Joe set the tone and paved the way. I do not think Joe even knows he is the ambassador that he truly is for The Divine. He just knows from the depth of his own being what I need to do next and somehow, he just makes it happen.

Which leaves me with the strange title of this chapter and today's journey. It is one thing to say something and intend it. It is quite literally another to set out and do what you say you are going to do. Accomplishing something scary and uncertain for me means I need to have faith and believe in a purpose much bigger than me. As I sit here in this big, empty house in the middle of Mexico in a community called Tequisquiapan, Tequis for short, in an attempt to write a book with a very heavy subject matter is, to say the least, a tad uncomfortable. I have titled this chapter "Mock Trial" for a reason. Do I have the courage to dig deeply and talk about a subject most of us try to avoid altogether? I have been saying I have to write this book, and yet my fear is deep. I am scared. I think, "Well, if I just make a practice run - a mock trial - then I can actually say to my Spiritual Father, I at least attempted to write about how it feels to come out of darkness and commit to working with Divine Spirit, encompassing light." Interesting, even as I write this I am sitting in darkness, and everyone in the community is still sleeping, or at least seems to be asleep.

At the beginning of January, Joe suggested we go to Mexico and spend a couple of weeks together in the warm weather. He made all the arrangements and we arrived on January 15th. We had a great time with our friends, while also spending a few quiet days just hanging out together. We walked every day and shopped for fresh ingredients at the local market. It makes me smile just thinking about how much we enjoy each other's company. But today was the day deep down I had been dreading and not talking much about. Today is the day Joe was leaving to go back home, leaving me alone here for a whole month to write a book.

I know some of you reading this, especially if you live in Canada or the northern part of the United States in February, might be thinking, "Poor you. You get to sit in a warm country and leisurely write a book." But consider this: despite claiming to be okay being totally alone and at peace with my Spiritual family, I was actually feeling pretty freaked out about being on my own in a country where I did not know many people or speak the language.

As Joe was preparing to leave to catch his ride to Queretaro Airport, a dear lady by the name of Carla offered to drive him for us. I walked him out to the car with a brave face, but a fearful heart. What in the heck did I think I was trying to accomplish? Who did I think I was? What did I possibly have to say that hundreds, or thousands, were not saying every day? Why didn't I just jump in that car beside Joe and stop this foolish notion of trying to support what I am called to support, and just throw in the towel and go back to my normal, everyday, safe life? All these thoughts were going through my head at 5:00 AM out on the dark street and returning to this empty space. So, I thought perhaps I could just attempt a mock trial chapter and see how I felt.

I am not going to lie. There are times when I know a client is really struggling and I pray I am offering the right love, healing information, facilitation, and channeling. There are times when I do not understand simple conversations about world matters and politics and famous people. Sometimes, I speak before I think! There is not a day goes by that I don't ask myself just who do I think I am, trying to make a small dent, a difference, while at the same time trying to live life to the fullest.

What I am trying to say here, even if I am giving myself a bit of a buffer by the tittle of this chapter, is that when you truly listen to the calling of your soul connections, if you allow yourself to think outside your comfort zone, you grow. Most people, myself included, would never leave or venture too far from home. As I wrote in my second book, I have come to understand on the deepest level that when you let your Spirit lead you to wholeness, truth, and honesty, there is just no room for complacency.

Tracey L. Pagana

As the dawn was starting to lighten the dark sky around the room, my sweet Joe texted to tell me he was about to get on the plane. He sent me this message, and it melted my heart: "I am at the airport. When you come home, they sell vanilla at the duty free by the gate if you want to pick some up here. I hope you rest today. You will be very tired. Remember, I am just a call away. XXOO." As he was boarding the plane for his journey back to his working world, I was feeling somewhat numb, lost, and sad. I know I said yes, and I felt honoured and blessed to have this opportunity, but I also felt challenged, being alone so far away from home. Divine Spirit had plans for me; I know this. I am ready and I said yes to the completion of my next task: coming out of darkness and into to the light, with my eyes and heart wide open!

UNDER THE VEIL OF DARKNESS

Part One

Under the veil of darkness, if you look closely, you can see pinpricks of light poking through. This new light shows me, in colour, living examples of love. I would like to paint for you in this chapter my experience of these pinpricks of love seeping through the cracks.

I had the good fortune to be able to write most of this book in Mexico. My sweet Joe planned for me to have a block of time to myself to write. As I was writing, the previous chapter stirred up many tears of shame, addressing deep toxins that came to the surface and needed releasing. I decided to go into town for a long walk, to clear my mind and my heavy heart and to release and forgive myself on a deeper level, breathing in the cool mountain air.

I started thinking about the three Catholic Sisters I had asked a week ago for a blessing, and this made me smile. The Sisters spoke Spanish, of course, and so, I boldly walked up to them and asked in English for a blessing by pointing to them and making the Sign of the Cross. Well, it was magical! They all joined in the blessing. They spoke from their hearts, their souls, and their eyes. I could see their deep commitment and love for Jesus and God, The Father in them, in their actions, and in their words. Underneath their veils was a passion and a love for the cause they had committed to. I could see by their faces; their choices had not been easy. I could feel the struggle the three of them had had in their decisions, experiencing poverty, tackling obstacles, and, I can only assume, also addressing dark energy throughout over 36 years of service on their journeys. At the end of the blessing, I heard one Sister say in English, "May you go in peace and love." At that point, the tears started to slide down my cheeks, and I could see water pooling at the corner of their eyes, as well. Yes, it was a Father Spirit moment of Trinity. I hugged each one and kissed their cheeks, and I thanked them and quickly left them to give thanks for the miracle of love I had just received. Under the veil of darkness, always, you will find light if you seek it out.

I thought about that the following day as I was quietly walking into town. The previous evening, I had spent a wonderful evening with a kind, friendly woman I had met briefly on our last trip to Mexico. We had exchanged information and had checked in with each other throughout the year. She had asked me to let her know when we come back to Tequis and she would catch up with me. True to her word, GinaLinn reached out and invited me out to a book club gathering. It was amazing to be surrounded by a group of women ranging from 35 to 60 years old. I could not understand much, but two ladies, GinaLinn and Rachel, spoke English and kept me in the loop as the discussion ranged from heated verbal passion to tears and laughter. It was apparent these amazing women had a bond much like our Healing Circle in Canada. Everyone who entered the room not only hugged and kissed the others, but also extended the same sincere gestures to me, a stranger in their circle who could not even speak their language. These women, all of them, attempted to communicate from their hearts and genuine smiles. Under the veil of darkness, there are always pinpricks of light if you take the time and the courage to search them out.

Since the book club meeting was a ladies' night out, there was ample to eat and drink. I met a very elegant lady named Betty, who had brought a dish of tiny white homemade cookies sprinkled with icing sugar. I picked one up to take a bite, and it almost disintegrated into a mouthful of yumminess with a flavour I could not identify. Well, if I was not in total 'like' with Betty before the cookie, she sure had my attention now. We started a conversation about her and her baking, and she told me she owned a small shop called Chocolateria Fina. I asked for directions, and she handed me a map and told me she would be open only on Saturday, Sunday, and Monday that week, explaining that she goes out into the desert to gather ingredients to create special flavors in her handmade chocolates. On my way into the centre of the town, I decided to go on a quest to find her shop. Father Spirit had other plans for me, as under the veil of darkness there are pinpricks of light if you are brave enough and open enough to walk the path of where the light may lead you.

In the centre of the town square, there is a huge, beautiful Church, and I made a point daily to stop in and pray, sending out love, peace, and healing for both my physical and Spiritual families. It has become a habit now, and I feel very connected in this sacred space. This day was no exception. There is always someone in this space showing respect and reverence in deep their faith. It saturates and permeates my whole entire person. These are my Christian roots, and in this sacred solace, there is no boundary or language barrier, only a united peace. I do not practice my faith in the way I did as a child, as my God is bigger than any structure; however, I can always find the Trinity and the community of my childhood in a way that gives me great joy anywhere I feel God's essence.

As I entered the Church, the Priest was at the entrance, accompanied by a young altar boy. The Priest greeted me as I asked in English for a blessing from him. He led me over to the side of the Church, out of the way of traffic, and made the Sign of the Cross to bless me. His blessing was personal and deeply felt by both of us. Again, I was able to show deep gratitude through healing tears flowing down my cheeks. His eyes, like the eyes of the Sisters before him, started to pool as well. I went into the sanctuary of his house of love to give prayers and thanks. On my way out, a tiny Mexican woman spoke to me in Spanish. I tried to tell her I did not understand her, and then I heard on my heart, "Just show her she is loved." So, I pulled her tiny body close to mine and planted a big kiss right in the middle of her forehead. Her smile was communication enough for both of us. Under the veil of difficulty, poverty, darkness prevails. In these times, look beyond for these tiny holes of life experience to see the goodness in the light.

I left the Church somewhat in a daze of love that filled my heart. I walked towards my destination, not really knowing how to find Betty's shop, but feeling pulled to walk in a certain direction. It was like my heart was being directed and my feet were to follow. On the way, I stopped and asked a couple for directions and was told I was about 20 minutes in the wrong direction of my destination. I switched streets and continued my journey. I came upon two young girls, named Indi and Daisy, who were looking perplexed. They tried to direct me, I tried to direct them, and then Spirit hit me and I stopped the discussion as it was reflecting anxiety of all three of us trying to find our way. Under the veil of discouraging darkness, the light began to shine in their eyes. I asked them to hold hands and, without hesitation, I put my hands on each one of their hearts and started to sing to their hearts from Spirit, right on the spot, in the street, as they responded with full acceptance of the gift I too received from their hearts. I gave them each a huge violet breath to fill them and encourage them, sharing with them that they were surrounded by Spirit-filled protection and would find their way. We hugged and said goodbye.

Not one block later, still lost, I turned down a street I felt pulled to walk, and another very young girl met me. I stopped to ask for directions, and immediately she pulled out her phone to Google the address. We had no luck, but the conversation quickly turned into her despair of being in pain and lost. It was obvious to me in that moment of deep truth that she had a dark veil of energy around her heart that was causing doubt and clouding her direction. She told me she was a struggling writer trying to find her way. With her beautiful eyes, full of fear, pain, and self-doubt, my heart melted. I grabbed her, embraced her, and immediately started to clear her dark energy with Reiki as she allowed me, a stranger, to love her. Tears streamed down her face, and as I wiped them away, I felt the need to kiss her and hold her. I also breathed several breaths of loving, Spirit-filled energy into her, to renew her, give her hope, and teach her how to accept the love that would help her override the darkness and fear that seemed to be consuming her. As we walked away from each other, I was no further ahead in reaching my destination, but my Father Spirit was leading me to where he wanted me to be. With a smile, I moved on.

This is the best part of this whole chapter! I ended up at a coffee/chocolate shop I had been to before. It was familiar to me, and I stopped at the patio to ask if anyone spoke English. Yes! Finally! Two people spoke up, an elderly lady and a young lady who was having lunch with her parents. Since I was closer to the young lady, I asked if she could possibly help me with my destination. She was a great help. In fact, her parents both jumped in, leaving their meal to offer to find the place I was looking for. We had a great conversation about her schooling, and I shared some of the messages I was receiving for her and offered her some Reiki for her heart and her anxiety around exams and studying. She accepted, and after a short time delivering energy, I left them and went on my way. Can you believe Betty's chocolate shop was less than 200 yards past the patio I was just at and right around the corner? Under the veil of ignorance, there is always a Spirit-filled lesson of love.

Once at Betty's shop, I purchased a large supply of chocolate, which I quickly sampled. It was a beautiful experience and a nice reward from Spirit for being an obedient student and never doubting how I was to arrive at my destination in the way Spirit was directing me. The young lady Betty had hired to run her shop was incredibly competent. I gave her a tip for speaking English so well and assisting me. She was overjoyed, saying it was her very first tip. I felt happy when I left, on a cloud, rejoicing in everything I had experienced that afternoon. As an afterthought, I hurried back to Betty's shop and asked the young lady to pick out three of her favourite chocolates and put them in a separate bag. I was wishing with all my heart, as I hurried back to the patio, that the family would still be enjoying their lunch. They were joyfully eating and conversing, and I walked up to them quietly and discreetly handed the young girl, who had been so sweet, the bag containing the three chocolates as a thank you for being so kind and accommodating to me. The young girl at first refused my gesture, but at my insistence, she accepted. She then told me that she was shy and had never been open to allowing to anyone helping her in the way I had. In fact, the act was awkward and foreign to her; yet she felt what she was receiving deeply and felt free, energized, and "different." We hugged, and I gave her another violet breath on her heart to seal her healing. We thanked each other, and I went on my way.

As I continued my way back to the town centre, to find a few things for nourishment of my body, I realized that my day was all about soul nourishment. I gained rewards for being a diligent listener, an agent for Spirit, following a path that was not a clear route to my original destination. I ended up in the right place at the right time to help other souls searching for love and light. It was an honour to trust that Spirit had work for me to do, as well as rewards for me to appreciate. I was rich in body and Spirit and was able to easily find my way home. I stopped to buy a few things I needed at the market and treated myself to some beautiful yellow flowers to brighten the condo. Three times I almost gave them away on the way home. Three times a voice whispered on my heart, "No, Tracey! You need to receive as well as to give. These flowers are for you to enjoy. As you spend time reflecting on the day, find the joy in the balance of giving as well as receiving."

I am so grateful for this Spirit-filled day and the opportunity to share the story with you. As you continue to process your own personal veil of darkness, have a peek beyond the veil and set your eyes on all the light you get to experience. Every second of breath given to you is a gift!

UNDER THE VEIL OF DARKNESS

Part Two

The day after my trip to Betty's shop, I woke feeling very heavy; a result, I am sure, of the intensity of writing and the healing it can bring. I was truly missing my Joe. In all truth, we had not spent a whole lot of time apart. I felt a sense of loneliness, being apart from someone who just fits into your life so beautifully that you take it for granted. This experience was a huge deal for both of us.

When I did not hear from Joe that morning, I began writing the previous chapter, feeling the heaviness of the veil of darkness and loneliness that can sneak up on you. I brushed it off and kept writing. Joe called around 10:00 AM. He had slept in, and I was happy to hear he had taken the extra time out that his body needed. We chatted while he made coffee. He made me smile as he told me how domesticated he was becoming, buying a nice new comforter, and doing laundry. He told me what he planned on doing for the day, and I told him if I did not make an effort to get out of the house daily, there could be a real chance I could probably turn into a hermit. He agreed, and I got up and went for a long walk into town.

As I said that day, my body was in actual pain. Talking about darkness and writing about it, feeling it, can cause physical pain, and it is important to find ways to release the toxins. My back hurt all the way into town, and I remembered a conversation with my friend Dana, who speaks Spanish. She reminded me of the need to take care of myself while I was away and told me that if I needed help negotiating a price for a massage, she would help me to negotiate the price. I could simply hand her the phone, and she would do the negotiating. The thought of a massage made me feel warm inside. It was exactly what I needed, and as I turned toward the town centre, I passed a sign advertising mani-pedis. A young woman was standing outside handing out flyers in Spanish, advertising the restaurant inside. I made a gesture with my hands, like massaging, and she said led me indoors.

The next face I saw was a face I recognized. Her name was Ana and she had been at the book club gathering the previous week. It was her first book club meeting as well, as she had just moved to the area, and she told me she worked at the place which was a salon and restaurant all in one. I shared with her my desire for a massage and she immediately called the practitioner, who was on her way. Ana then made me a cup of herbal tea and started to share her personal journey, her broken life, and what led her to Tequis. As she talked, I shared healing energy on her heart, helping her release a veil of dark energy she needed to let go of. All the scars she was holding in her heart chakra started to release, and I was able then to sing for her in the quiet of the spa. We both shed healing tears, releasing together the pain and stress she had suffered.

The massage practitioner, Ceci, came in, and I must say, her technique was different than any other massage I have ever experienced. She lit a candle, put on her iPod, and asked me to lie on my back. Most massage experiences I have had in the past have been first lying on my stomach and flipping over. This massage lasted almost two full hours. I got lost as she not only massaged out all the stress, but also applied magic to pressure points I did not even know I had on my toes, my fingers, my glands, my ears. At one point, I thought it may just be a one-sided massage; however, she eventually asked me to roll over from my back to my stomach and started to work all the accumulated pain out of my back. Ceci worked for over an hour, getting me relaxed enough to let go in a way that was less painful than attacking the most pain-filled part of body my back. Because she had taken the time to work all the stress and tightness out, relaxing even my facial muscles along my jawline, I was able to endure what had to be worked out of my back. I was a puddle of mush when she finished and said not a word, leaving me to get dressed at my leisure. I was able to shed all the stress that had built up as I wrote of pain that had been buried under my own veil of darkness.

When I came out of the treatment room, to my surprise three women were waiting for me: Ana, who I had met Friday night and who recognized me when I had first arrived; Ceci, my massage therapist; and Michelle, the owner of the salon. They were talking quietly and waiting for me to join them. Ana grabbed my hand and pulled me towards her boss, Michelle. Ana introduced us, and I took Michelle's hands, looked into her eyes, and spoke to her heart as we shared a sacred moment as Father Spirit spoke to her heart. I then took Ceci's hands, and we also shared a very sacred message to her heart from Father Spirit. It was a magical, reverent, sacred time together. We then held hands as I sang from my soul to these women, who were thirsty to find the source of this well of free, connected Spirit. We had no words, just the experience of true, unconditional love, breaking barriers of language in that moment. Ana called it magic, and, in a way, she is correct. The Source I work for is white light magic that can melt a veil of darkness, clearing out the shadows lacking self-love. In that union, white light is invited into dark, empty spaces, filling those spaces with new light, new hope, new birth.

The three women then invited me to an open house at Michelle's shop on Thursday night, and to share in a circle of love, messages, healing energy, prayer, and gratitude. I, of course, said accepted the invitation. After all, I am here to bring the Source I work for into the darkness and into the hearts of people who are craving something more. Knowledge is power, and power is right inside your very own space. We are those pinpricks of light who work for Source. It is our job, in our awareness, to be open to

Tracey L. Pagana

where and why Source may be leading you, perhaps down an alley straight into a small shop. You need to trust in all you are and be ready to be that light. Shine like you know why you are shinning, and always choose love to guide your path.

SAINT VALENTINE

Saint Valentine was a widely recognized 3rd Century Roman saint, commemorated in Christianity on February 14. From the High Middle Ages his Saints Day has been associated with a tradition of courtly love.

Jack is seven, a modern-day saint and although he cannot quite comprehend why, he let me share his story and paint this picture for you. He truly is a saint in the most modest, innocent, way. Is that not how all saint's start out? Living from the core of their passionate hearts and leading by example?

Lori his mom is someone I have gotten to know on a personal level over the past several years. Her story is not mine to tell but, I can tell you she is so aware of the bigger picture, really caring, creative and a kind, intelligent person. She is also the mother of three children, a girl and two boys.

When Lori found out I was going to Mexico she had discussed her desire of wanting me to bring some of her creations with me to give out to children. Mini wooden painted animated toys, some animals, some human, some intended to replicate characters in children's shows. She makes each one of them with love. All of them are meticulously and delicately hand painted, a labour of love. Some of these fine features I am sure took serval hours of tiny brush strokes.

So, when she called me before I left for Mexico with Joe and then to start writing this book it was because she wanted me to take some of these figurines with me. Jack, had a talk with his mom saying, "Please send some Mom and Tracey can find poor children who do not have any toys to give them too so they can have something special from us."

If you think this was touching wait, until I tell you what Jack did next. He not only took sixteen sets which he picked out himself, but then went and got his personal singing bowl, drum, stick and blessed the dolls himself. When Lori dropped of this bag of love to my house and sent me the picture of Jack praying over the toys through a message, I knew in my heart they had to end up somewhere very special. I was on a mission to find the perfect people to receive Saint Jack's love.

For almost three weeks I thought about where they should end up. I would walk into town everyday bringing one or two with me, but never felt called to give them to anyone I encountered on my daily walks around the town. I asked my new acquaintances and my friends who live there now, and they all offered up great ideas. I finally decided I would take the whole bag of love with me and visit an orphanage on the outskirts of town.

Sometimes the best laid plans have other Divine intervention, and this was no exception. I was having coffee with GinaLinn, a beautiful person inside and out. She said, "You know Tracey I just had a thought occur to me. I know you had talked about the orphanage, bringing those special toys but the book club I belong to is making cookies and home-made treats, bringing them to our old age home tomorrow. I just had this thought that old people in places like that revert back to children and would absolutely love those precious hand painted gifts. In fact, they could put them in their rooms and look at them and they would make them smile." When Spirit spoke to GinaLinn's heart it presented a fantastic idea.

Excited about the day, I woke up early. I was a little lonely missing my Joe and started to write the chapter I had laid out in my head before the sky started to lighten. The sun never came out and the cloudy sky stated to threaten a not very pretty Valentine's Day. This did not detour my plans or dampen my Spirits, in fact, I did not even notice the dark sky. I finished my chapter and headed out the door around 12:15 only to discover the gray was gone and the sun was shining.

I had written down the address that GinaLinn had provided me as well as a Spanish translation on where I was from and what I wanted to give the residents. I was off to find my senior's home. Father Spirit is so good to me. He sent me on a path into town and I ran into a nice young artist who has her own shop. I had met her the day before adjoined to Ellie's coffee shop we chatted for a moment, her English impeccable said your friend from San Antonio is at the coffee shop. Right away I knew she was talking about Flor who I had met initially at the Friday night book club and who is a dear friend of GinaLinn.

The coolest thing was as all of this was being directed by Divine Source. I was praying all the way into town that I would be able to find my way to the senior home. I entered the coffee shop, saw Ellie and Flor right away and we hugged and said good morning. Flor had just finished her lunch, and was just chatting with a few other women, offered me a seat to join her at her table. We started a conversation. I asked her if she would be able to help me find my way to deliver the gifts. I had a piece of paper that GinaLinn, God bless her heart, had taken the time to send it to me via text providing me the address in Spanish as well as a paragraph in Spanish. GinaLinn took the time to explain to the staff stating in the paragraph introducing me: This is Tracey, from Canada, she brings gifts of love to offer the people that live here. The gifts she is giving you have been blessed by a little boy.

Flor read the address and the note and said "I am going in that direction I would be happy to walk with you." I was elated and said I would be very grateful for the help and then I had a thought, I said "Flor you are welcome to join me in the experience and share it with me if you like." You could tell she was thinking about it and said "I do not really have any plans but to go to the store so, yes, I would like to do that." In all the commotion I was taking out the little figurines and showing the women out of the corner of my eye a young, women with a pretty smile approached me and said may I see.

She introduced herself with the prettiest name Alejandrina "Alexandria" as she extended her hand and it landed in mine, I felt her powerful loving energy. It was a spark we both felt between us like a bolt of electricity we both knew it was a conductor from Divine Spirit. When I told her about Jack and his story and the love his mother Lori extended her eyes started to water. She told me that she worked with children as a life coach, and spending many weeks taking these same children on educational camping trips, at her parents, hacienda (a parcel of land like a small hobby farm) in the mountains. These excursions lasted three weeks at a time, with sixty children and a team she hired of twenty to teach them. She did the pre work and continued working with them on a program built specifically around these children's needs, both before and after the camping trips. Teaching them how to be more in tune with themselves building healthy boundaries, new awareness, and self-esteem. Alejandrina used to work with adults but now has built her own business around supporting the health and wholeness of children. You could see and feel the passion, and responsibility she felt for these young people.

Alejandrina then did the most incredible thing, she took my hand and led me into her little store adjacent to the coffee shop at the back. She wanted to match what Jack gave and proceeded to give me sixteen premade packages all done up with yellow and green ribbon in clear cellophane bags. They contained a small colouring book, a special tool when you pressed the page colour would appear on the paper and colourful plasticine for molding, something which would be so therapeutic for arthritic hands. You could feel the gift oozing from her beautiful heart. We both got emotional as we made our way back out to the body of the terrace of the coffee shop. We had made a connection and we both knew we had.

Flor offered me a ride instead which I appreciated now that I had a heavy bag of gifts. Ellie's mother was the one that offered us the ride as she was just leaving as well. Both Flor and I were grateful as the destination we were headed was quite a bit farther to walk then we had anticipated. When we arrived, we thanked Elinor, and stepped out of the car to this beautiful baritone's voice serenading the residents in a special Valentine's Day concert. We waited for the song to end and then a worker with a pretty smile and sparkling eyes approached us. I did not have to do any of the talking as Flor was very kind to do it for me. I could hear her introducing me and sharing why we were there. She handed the worker my note that GinaLinn had complied to further explain why we were there with a bag full of gifts. What happened next has me still in awe.

We waited outside the recreation hall in the terrace area until the singer finished his next song. Flor had asked how many were in the room and together we made sure we had something for each of them. We had to do a bit of rearranging, but it all worked out and we had 44 items ready to give everyone who were seated in a big circle inside. We were then introduced to the residents. Sometimes you just know by the flow, Divine Spirit was in full swing, like watching dominos falling in perfect order creating the perfect scenario.

After the introduction I went around the room giving everyone a gift. I was not ready for the gift of love I received back. Every one of these beautiful souls gave me a huge hug and a kiss. As tears streaming from their eyes started the flow of tears in mine. I could feel the love and gratitude deeply and they touched my face as they received the gifts each one of them talking to me in their beautiful Spanish. I could literally see the small child returning from where they were born so many years ago, returning to the root of all of them displaying the full life they lived. Returning to their child full circle initiated by a seven-year-old boy, far across the ocean several thousand miles away. Saint Jack, look what your love, your calling and your Spirit started. How very special a boy you truly are. Flor was gracious enough to stand back and let me deliver all the gifts I offered but she declined, in her grace and elegance took photos so when I get back home, I could share them with Jack and his mother. I asked the singer if I could borrow his microphone and spoke in English saying I do not speak Spanish but would like to sing to you in English. After I sang a blessing of love, they all got up out of their chairs and sang back a Spanish blessing to both of us.

We said goodbye and floated out of the building walking through a neighborhood that Flor proudly says are her people. Rural, down to earth community of simple elegance, friendly blue collar, hardworking people. You can feel her pride for them, and their own self pride. She showed me the area a couple of her favorite eateries, as we continued to both walk together back to the main street. We hugged and she said that made her day special and I said mine to. She went on to do errands I continued back into town.

I felt pulled back to the coffee shop to share the story and the photos of the joyful experience to what Alejandrina had provided so many people that day. We talked for quite a while her sharing her life, me sharing mine, and how Spirit directed the events of the powerful day. We felt beyond blessed for having the exchange together. I left knowing we will work together in the future in some capacity.

Later, after I got home and was recovering from the deep emotional energy the day had set, I reached out to Lori thinking by chance she may be home. She was and so was Jack. She called him over to the phone and my heart gushed out telling them both about the events of the day and how I had prayed very hard for the direction of Jack's intentions in Mexico. You could tell he was a bit perplexed why the older people received his gift of love and not the children he intended them for. But I could also feel his happiness that they went to special people that needed to feel the love from a child. His mother responded to me a while after and said that after she explained to him that older people can sometimes go back to be childlike in their hearts and that they will treasure the gifts they received; he was beaming.

Jack, who we will forever dub Saint Jack, left his mark on many hearts February 14, 2020. Alejandrina texted me later in the evening saying she was thinking about Jack and that he is certainly special. Yes, that says it best certainly Jack is special.

Valentine's Day can be a day of sadness for many people. This special holiday has developed social status, gaining popularity designated in celebrating love, but also making a great deal of money. This promotes a subliminal expectancy that your love may not be enough unless, you purchase something special to prove your love. If your own expectations of this holiday do not work out, it can make you sad or even a bit depressed, especially if you are alone or struggle with being alone. Again, the darker energy subjects these expectations. Greed of the industry needing to expand financially gaining wealth in some ways even taking advance in the exploitation of love. This greed, this power, sneaks into a very sacred intended day of love and kindness, we share with and for each other. However, there are still saints, and the experience of living among them that provide you the teaching and the experience that Jack provided today. Pure innocence, pure intentional love, melting the hearts of forty-four seniors, spreading and infecting way beyond that. All of us had the joy in the receiving and the giving, a seven-year- old earth angel provided. This experience will live on in our hearts for years to come.

Out of the darkness a modern-day saint, with the name Jack, shared a connection with a 3rd Century Roman Saint from High Middle age. These two saints joining in the celebration of love on the day of the year most recognized for love!

WEARING POSITIVE ENERGY ON YOUR SLEEVE

As I sit in the quiet reflection of yet another gorgeous day in the middle of the Mexican mountains, the peaceful state of this still sleeping little town it is easy to be positive. It's been one full month plus two days since arriving here. Being positive is not something that comes natural to many of us. It is a state of mind and a commitment to be consciously aware of every second, every moment, and every breath we take.

I have read on average that it takes more than two months before a new behavior becomes automatic, 66 days to be exact. Forming a habit that remains ingrained in you is habitual, consistent, and repetitive. I have also read It can take anywhere from 18 to 254 days for a person to form a new habit confirming my first read for the average of 66 days for a new behavior to become automatic. Our strong ego seems to want to fight against our human nature to avoid change, and motion that takes effort that may not feel like a normal function in our conscious way of living.

Change is hard. I am reminded of this as I pull out a half page of torn paper from my lap top storage case that I had written the in the first four days of adjusting here a month ago. This is what I had written verbatim:

Arrived Tuesday January 14th.
Did not even know how blocked and congested my body and heart chakra was. It has taken me four full days, four full nights to settle into full embodiment. I feel no peace, only tired lower frequency energy seeping in emotions of self-doubt. My life, the rat race of society, seems to keep me in a preputial state of motion, needs, and noise that keeps me from my discovery of true self.

Reading this note in a different light today than I had written the context of the note a month ago drove me to write about it today.

I would be lying to all of you if I did not admit how hard this book has been to write. Before I started writing the context, I sat down and wrote about 25 chapter titles. I thought that if I wrote down the titles that my Father Spirit would direct my heart, open my soul, and channel through. In some chapters that is exactly what did happen. In others, it was through pain and experience I wrote about coming out of personal dark experiences.

I decided when I came to Mexico to wear positive and healing energy on my sleeve every day. I intend it, just like my habit is to start the coffee pot even before I brush my teeth or make my bed. Coffee is my weakness for sure. So now, my new habit will be my mental intention. I ask to be surrounded in positivity. I ask for the energy to drench my whole state of awareness. I ask to be an open vessel of love for all things that are come my way in the day. I ask for a calm sense of order so that I can function through any drama, life of loss, hope, and conflict. Tall order yes. Practically impossible, as we are all faced with disappointment, struggles, and difference of opinions. We all still need to intertwine with the people we love, and the friends we want to support. This takes vast amounts of energy.

Asking for this intention to become habitual works, however you still feel the brokenness of heartache and disappointment even deeper than you did before personal positivity started to form and gel sustaining its presence within your core. The more positive you become the more you are aware of the darkness and pain living through the connections and pain others experience. It is extremely hard to be positive when so many people cannot seem to find it. It is difficult to separate yourself from the emotions, pain or heartache that inflicts others that you love.

I have come to understand in a deeper way that my commitment to positive energy allows my vessel to engage, serving this energy. This understanding causes me to react differently when I am in the middle of a confrontational situation. It allows me to think past my own needs of wanting to fix and instead, allows me to consider it with loving essence, reacting less aggressively towards the emotional infernal growing in the confrontation. This new perspective of quiet positivity infects my whole being providing a calm strength. This strength teaches me insight such as knowing when to stay reflective, knowing when to offer silent prayer, knowing when to respond with words, and knowing when to take a form of action without words.

Sometimes when people are in conflict it only aggravates the situation more when another person wants to offer advice or ways to consider addressing their inner turmoil. If we are being honest, not one of us likes it when someone we love is hurting. It hurts us deeply and we just want that hurt to go away no matter what it takes. Being invested in your own positivity provides insight, wisdom, and understanding that sometimes the only thing that can fix pain is allowing the person who is in pain some privacy to work it out themselves. This requires taking a step back and really investing in your own truth so that you have the insight to see others. Respecting their growth, their pain, and their choices gives them the space to breathe.

How hard is this commitment? Who has not heard that we are a work in progress? Who, among you reading this has not really been listening? While in your brain thoughts have been forming a rebuttal of what you are hearing from the other, wanting to stake your claim on your own thought process. Is that love? Or is that just wanting to feel good about something you believe is the write answer, the solving of a problem, a way to feel self-inflated, claiming power of control just because you may very well be right does not make it right.

I have had a whole month in the state of grace and silence to reflect on all of this. There have been days this new silence was louder than the world I left behind. In this silence I have found the balance I have been trying to form for years. I have been able to find peace in this balance. This added ingredient has cemented a brand-new foundation within my internal home. This foundation has slowed me down, enough so that I might truly hear what I am called to be for everyone Spirit puts in my life. This new internal flow of positivity allows me to grieve with others, feel the growth with others, and accept that I do not have to give a piece of myself to anyone who is suffering. I don't have to feel sad, hurt, or involve myself in anything a lower frequency might be teaching others through in the lesson, unless, invited to share it with them. I have learned this last month the biggest gift I can give another in infliction and pain is to surround them in light.

Advice is something everyone I know wants to be a part of. It makes you feel good when another person asks for your wisdom, thoughts, healing, or confidence. It makes you feel powerful, and even in some circumstances invincible. However, not everyone is looking for advice, in fact some people just want you to send love and healing silently behind their curtain of privacy. This has been a very big lesson for me this past month. I have sent many intentions without having to talk about them. Spending many hours alone in silence, with Divine Spirit, in the house of Spirit, I have come to really understand the power of intentions. Sometimes my biggest moments of magic and connection have been in the commitment of this silence in the walls of the cathedral.

Positive over the top emotion can be as exhausting as dark energy. This may seem like a strange sentence so I will take some time to explain this. When a person is very emotional giving of self, receiving so much pure love, even the embrace of it, can literally causes real pain. To receive or even bearing witness to this kind of receiving can also be extremely exhausting. The energy is foreign to most people it's very hard for people to receive excess amounts of love and attention. We are not wired that way. We would rather be the person that does all the giving. We get to remain in control this way we have an order internally of controlling our emotions, this allows us the illusion of order. Or at least the possibility that order will keep us in a safe harbour within. As I have said many times, safety is an illusion, this is only a figment of your imagination. There is no safety, it you are going to live an honest life, addressing all your truth and all your emotions. When you wear positive energy on your sleeve, take the time to visually see what positive energy might look like descriptively as you proudly wear it. Become the listener you always knew you could be. Actions of kindness should be as natural as waking up and making your bed, preparing a cup of coffee, and brushing your teeth. These acts of kindness should feel like second nature. They will teach you every day how to grow wiser, stronger, and kinder. These acts of positive energy will teach you patience to accept who you are, better yet, love who you are yet to become. The biggest gift though, will teach you how to listen with your heart, instead of your ears.

May I be so bold as to candidly state that being nice, if it is authentic, takes a huge amount of commitment dedication, and personal sacrifice. For the good of wholeness, it is also at times a very lonely place to exist. Being nice is often not taken seriously and some people may even have trust issues if you appear to be nice. Awareness will help you reach this goal, as you will need to become the living example of kindness. The only way you will know you are on the right track to this habit, is to quietly commit to it. This may be even more painful than you can imagine as there are no shinny stars, or personal pedestals in this loving energy. There will be many times your prayers for others, your examples of selfless acts, and your courage go unnoticed. It is a quieter way of doing Divine Spiritual work for the sake of all the broken seeking whole self and love. As you grow into authentic kindness, you will need less from your earthly habitat and you will be privy to more Spiritual secrets. These secrets will be your new prana "soul food" providing space within that will remain your private place to contemplate all the things that have become sacred to you. We all deserve to elevate to this level of transitioning. Becoming one within your own highest power. This power allows you the privilege and honour to see both sides of the coin, remaining in a state of perfectly balanced peace.

The pearls will come, as well as all the shining moments that continue to build your portfolio. I have been saving this to put into the best spot in a chapter. It's from a client who shared her healing with me. I would like to share it with you I have her permission.

Hi Honey. Just wanted to let you know my Spirit is still holding on to and accepting the healing I received so lovingly from you yesterday. It's like I cannot be touched by the sadness and motion of existing living, existing energy swilling around me looking for a way in. It is being blocked by those two tall, beautiful beings standing behind my left shoulder. I feel their presence and power and my body still releasing old toxins and attachments. It is like I am bearing witness without attachment if that makes sense.

It is like I can separate myself from the personal attachment I was so familiar connecting too. It is like I can step out and listen and provide differently to just bear witness to the miracles of the moment, be the connector release the rest. Thank you.

It is like I am a dot in a picture, and you took a marker and connected to help me connect source differently. I hope this all makes sense. I feel calmer than ever before and ready for whatever is coming.

It is my job to deliver and facilitate source to the hungry. In the delivery the pearls of humbled appreciation appear, they keep aligning from source to source. These are moments that you know that you are doing your job and that your job is making a difference.

TOUCHED BY THE SPIRIT DURING A SPANISH MASS

This morning I slept in until 8:30 AM, I have not slept past 6:30 AM since coming to Mexico January 15. Although we are only I hour ahead of Mexican time in Canada, I am still in work mode here and it seemed like it was just time to get up. The sun was bright when I opened my eyes and stretched my arms and legs out in the laziest, biggest yawn. My sweet Joe did not call and wake me up as he thought I might be sleeping in. He was right, I have been writing in the wee hours before dawn for a little over two weeks now. In the morning I hear my Spirit, as it whispers my name and encourages the words to form from my soul, connecting to my heart, spreading to my fingers with a buzz of Spirit energy, then directly to my laptop.

I got up, it felt foreign not to still be in my pajamas, usually by this time I already had my second cup of coffee. Yes, I must confess, I have a slight coffee addiction. I always call my morning coffee, nectar of the Gods! In fact, that is usually Joe's first question before he starts any early morning conversation with me. "Honey have you had your coffee yet?" We both get a good chuckle from that comment. And to be honest I am a whole lot sweeter in disposition after I have had a cup, maybe even two.

So, as I said I was out of routine and it felt like this whole day might take on new direction, new meaning so with a happy heart and a smile on my face, I went in to take my shower and wash my hair. When I came out of the shower, I noticed that Joe had called me, and I had missed the call. I took a few moments to call him back and catch up on his night and morning. We, Joe and I had breakfast together over the phone it was very sweet. Technology is a gift providing me way of talking to Joe every day. Talking to Joe and seeing his face settles me. This helps me, to stay focussed on getting my work done, without missing my home life too terribly. I am so very lucky to have all this comfort and all this quiet time to work for my Spiritual Father. How very blessed I am to have all these options and all needs met.

I told Joe on the phone call that my heart was craving something special today, yes, every day I have found peace and joy and deep Spiritual connection in the church in the centre of the square. I feel so connected to Spirit, have deep conversations with Spirit, in the cool beautiful church. I send prayers up to everyone I am connected to be it family, friends, clients, requests, and special events. I usually arrive between 3PM-5PM to talk to my Spirit Father as well as say hello to anyone else doing the same.

I wanted to mention the sweetest moment one day last week. This little lady stopped by me when I was kneeling in prayer and was chatting away to me in Spanish I thought she wanted something like a coin or something else from me and was trying to ask her what she would like in my English she was still talking to me in Spanish, she had this smile that shone from her entire face. The man beside her said in broken English, "She wants nothing from you except to say to you: You are her amigo, she says she wants to be your friend. She likes your smiling face and the way you want to come here and pray with her people." What a message of love from the sweetest stranger, her Spirit mingling with my Spirit in her sacred home space. Wanting nothing but to be my friend.

I find the natives of Tequisquiapan sincerely genuine, simple, honest and intriguing, they try to speak English to me, I try to speak Spanish to them, neither of us getting very far, but we try to communicate. What I have noticed in this way of communication we both find other ways to work with our differences. We use objects, or tools, pictures, or gestures. These incredibly, diversified, intelligent, natives, not only share their home and space with me they make me feel welcome everywhere I go.

I felt called to go to Mass today, although raised Catholic, I have not been to mass on a regular basis for many years. This is not out of disrespect, not one bit, as I am very comfortable going to any Church or house of God and never feeling out of place. I find God everywhere I go in every moment I breathe. But last night I truly had a desire to wake up, walk into town and go to Mass.

I fixed my hair and put on the prettiest dress I brought. I wanted to be respectful of the tradition here. This place has an unspoken dress code, I think this unspoken code has a lot to say about these simple kind people, and the respect they have for their bodies. The women always wear skirts, blouses, pants, capris, no short shorts or revealing shirts. The men always wear nice shirts, collared shirts, and long pants.

As I walked into town today dressed for church, I also wore, a big smile on my face. It was such a beautiful day to be out in the world with the warmth of the sun in the early morning I felt like something really, special, was about to take place for me.

I got to the centre of town where the big church stands about 9:20 AM. I noticed as I approached the side of the church were the little Chapel attached to the church in connection to the bigger structure a whole mass had congregated at the entrance listening to the Priest ending the first mass of the morning, it touched my heart, the faith of these people with no more room inside the church they stood in droves outside its walls. As I walked around the entrance at the front of the church the same thing a mass of about another 50 faith filled people praying outside as there was no room inside. Some of the women held rosaries between their fingers. I tried not to stare at them for their commitment of love to Mary as their lips moved in prayer working the beads with their fingers all the while listening to the speaker outside the church of the priest, mixing with the congregation's responses. How absolutely full my heart got watching and listening as I ducked inside the entrance. The crowd was oblivious, and not ashamed who looked on or at them as they stood in dedicated respect, showing unabashed love of their faith. This connection these people have and the love and respect they have made me even more emotional. I did not hide my tears nor did they.

The mass continued, I did not understand one word, yet I understood every single gesture of love, respect, reverence in every word and action. I felt, more than I understood, the language was not a barrier. Our Spirit our unity as one in communion, there were no boundaries, only unity for one God and all his beloved children, we all belonged to him in that hour, in that mass, sharing his body, his blood, his son, and the Trinity of Spirit.

The other thing that absolutely fascinated me was the interaction with the Priest and congregation. I was transfixed during the sermon the priest included his people, he asked questions, they answered him in one voice, all responding to his questions. There was laughter, talking, humor, responses to humor, there was obviously a huge connection going on between the priest and his people. The shepherd, leading his sheep, by allowing the human element of collaborated connection. They were committed, engaged, he was leading and teaching. This was extremely powerful. This priest was brilliant, he was teaching his people that we are all worth so very much, his actions cemented the message of love. The peace be with you had everyone offering hands and hugs, no strangers in the house of father Spirit. All one family no one sees flesh just Spirit.

I received communion. I felt like I was being pulled out of my seat and found myself in the line. I did not feel even though it has been many years receiving this blessed, sacrament I was not worthy. I felt like I was getting a gift, of faith, of truth, of Trinity love. I just kept hearing as kneeled in reverence and prayer as the wafer slowly melted, disintegrating in my mouth, you need to receive, over and over I heard this on my heart, my soul, as my eyes welled again in total gratitude of this rich reward.

To say I floated out of the entrance doors leading the way down to the market without noticing if my feet hit the ground would be pretty accurate. I might not have been totally connected back in the whole sense of my body until the man at the vegetable stand gave me a price of the items I had just purchased. I started to regain all my motor skills and resumed the routine of my day.

I bought a chicken, came home changed my clothes, made soup, and picked up my computer to attempt even trying to come close to counting all the blessing of my day. It's now early evening, the birds are still rejoicing and singing about their own days, the sun is starting the ritual of the setting here. Its 6:35 PM it's still perfectly warm with a very gently breeze tickling the back of my neck and the strands of hair around my face.

I am so entirely grateful to have had this day, my life today was gifted with high mass sharing love and genuine kindness with people who adore their faith, their heritage, and their tradition. I hope and pray that this remains embedded in my heart for many years. Touched by the Spirit, one loving energy held in the space of this Spanish Mass. I appreciate it with all I am that the shadow of darkness stays clear of this space. Thus, giving way for the sun to shine in through the cracks and windows of the church walls, surrounding us in the gathering that today's actions gifted me.

FROM DARKNESS TO LIGHT

GOD HAS YOUR BACK

I was walking home from the centre square of the town, when a pleasant looking young man walked up to me, wanting to know if I would like to purchase his cupcakes. He had two in the box left for sale. He addressed me in initially in Spanish, smiled and quickly switched to English. He was on mission to sell the last two so, he pitched, and I listened.

His name was Marco. Marco was trying to make extra income. After having a brief conversation and purchasing the last two cupcakes, I asked him to please give them away to where he felt called to give them. I asked him to consider giving them to someone hungry. I invited him to sit with me on a bench out of the way of the main traffic on a side street. We talked about how he ended up here, what he did for a living, and then he shared deeper. I left the bench after we hugged. He went his way; I continued my way.

This young man's face and struggles stayed with me. I could not shake him. I had offered to exchange information, and he suggested we do a session together. I agreed before talking it over with Joe. When I got home Joe and I had a conversation about this young man and about giving him a session. Joe, in his wisdom, said "Tracey, you know why you have been given this time and this gift. You know that you are supposed to write this book. Stay focussed, as you have this job to complete and that you have been called out to write."

I reached out to Marco leaving him a message stating that I was sorry, but I could not meet with him for a session. I had to stay focused on what I was here to do but did say I would be back next year and would absolutely see him for a session at that time. I then told him I would send him love and prayers to encourage him to stay strong on his mission of self-discovery. I asked him to reach out to me when he needed anything, and that we would stay connected.

Marco did not respond back to me until the next day, as he was out late. Out of consideration he did not want to wake me at the late hour and apologised for not returning my message. I was so impressed at his consideration. He understood my commitment and respected why we could not have a session. Marco thanked me and continued to say that he felt Spirit had connected us to meet, and that he was grateful for the gifts we shared. He then told me he would stay in touch.

Well, Spirit had other plans for the two of us. Saturday morning, I met my girlfriend in the square. As we chatted about girl stuff, I happened to notice Marco walking our way. I yelled out to him with a big smile, and he walked over our way. We hugged each other as he presented his empty box proudly proclaiming that he had sold all his cupcakes. He extended his hand to Kathi for introduction. We talked for a few more minutes and he was off. Still feeling in my heart that we had unfinished business, I let it go and carried on in my day spending it with my friend having a great adventure

Just before I wake up in the morning, is when I usually hear Spirit the loudest. This morning I heard "reach out to Marco today." Marco responded with a voice message and throughout the course of the next hour shared together the real reason we were to meet for the third time. Yes, you know that the Trinity shows up all the time when these occurrences happen. Like clockwork, Divine intervention shows up and puts a plan into perpetual motion. After realizing what Spirit intended, Marco and I discussed the best option on his chapter brainstorming on my end, accepting what would work best on his. We decided that I would write the beginning of this chapter, Marco would write the body and I would conclude the ending. My feeling, writing his story, everyone courageous enough to tell his or her story deserves to tell it in their own way. He deserves this healing with the power of his own words, describing the life choices he made. This allows a deeper healing. Courage to talk about it is an opportunity to heal within. The next part of this book will be written from the hand and heart of this courageous young man. Be patient with him, he has a lot to say. It is the first time he has released so much personal information. He cried, was physically sick to his stomach, broke out in sweat, released anxiety, as well as the fear of being rejected in his words. This took a huge dedication of personal time, honesty and not holding back. He has been asked to write his story many times by many people. But he chose now to do it. Grab a cup of hot tea, a blanket, maybe even a box of Kleenex as this brave young man tells his story.

Marco's story:

It was the morning of December 17th, 2007 and I was 17. I was preparing to go to school when my mom told me that my dad had just had a stroke. The next day, my brother and I got on a plane to go and see him in the hospital. The moment I saw my father, my hero, full of tubes placed on his body, assisting his life support, was the most profound, impactful, moment of my life. After the stroke, my dad was unable to speak. He just was not the same person I had known before his stroke. It felt like he had abandoned me. Being the oldest made me feel it was my responsibility to restore him to his previous self. But he did not want to, he would not put in the effort. I believe in a way he liked being in that condition because of all the attention he received, his unconscious mind did not let him recover. Whatever tools of support to assist his recovery he rejected, in fact, he made it his mission to remain in the same condition without any trace of improvement. I wanted the opposite of course, so I suffered a lot. It's the same thing with an addict. There is nothing the family can do until the addict decides to do something about his own choices. I know that by my own experience.

My Father was an addict, a coke head, a crack head, an alcoholic who would constantly go to brothels and have sex with prostitutes, all the while having two kids and a wife at home. My mom, an ignorant town girl, who did not know anything about drugs became more and more anxious due to his absence in our home. Being from Mexico, not knowing any English, and residing so far from her home country, my mother felt helpless and did not know what to do. Her anger, frustration, and anxiety were released on both myself and my brother. I remember when how I felt when I was made aware of this information about my father it left me wounded, betrayed, and disgusted. I did not understand how my mother could be with such a man.

It's no coincidence I started smoking after my dad suffered a stroke. Getting high was what I had chosen to numb the pain.

And my path into darkness begins.

I would go every day to school high and I lived for the weekends. All I cared about was being liked by people. I would naturally observe people who were good with people at social gatherings, learning the examples set by my father from a very early age. I perfected this by going to parties, drinking, and smoking. I developed a mask, a completely fake mask. I was broken, immature, insecure and desperate for people's approval, yet I wore this mask of confidence so well that even though deep down I somehow knew the truth, I chose to believe that my mask was my real self. In truth that is what arrogance is, a lie. I lied to myself and I believed in the lies to protect me from my painful truth.

Using alcohol and marijuana helped me develop this mask to its fullest potential. I was able to reconnect with popular kids that had tossed me aside during middle school, and now because of partying and getting high with them they had accepted me again. I felt victorious. My whole life I had been shy, quiet, and anti-social and deemed weird by poplar kids. I would pride myself that I could go into a party without knowing hardly anyone, and leave knowing everyone.

Time started to go by. I graduated high school, did not get into any college outside of my city because, I was so lazy I did not apply to college. During that summer of my high school graduation, I met and fell in love with a girl. Everything was right in the world. We had just graduated high school, I was with my best friends daily partying, and I was with the love of my life and not a worry in the world. We started taking more mushrooms and ecstasy.

Tracey L. Pagana

Next semester I started College in my hometown. I got into a fraternity, tried LSD and cocaine. LSD for me, is very similar to weed with the added, bonus of hallucinating entering an altered dimension. So, obviously I fell in love with it as well. Now I understood why hippies were hippies and why the used the combination of weed and LSD. I would constantly tell everyone too that "tomorrow" I was going to stop for good. Five days later when I got caught smoking, they would ask me "Hey I thought you were going to stop, what happened?" That semester was the only one I have ever finished for college. That was in December 2009

2010 was when everything changed. I entered my 3rd stage of addiction.

This was the moment I started using drugs to not feel bad, instead of using drugs to feel good. Before I would do ecstasy once every month or two months, now it became a weekend thing. Taking mushrooms on a Friday night, mixing mushrooms with ecstasy and weed, mixing LSD with alcohol, and weed, mixing ecstasy with LSD. All, of the above. But what really hit me was that I had lost the respect of my friends. It was not the same anymore. I had a group of close friends that lived in the same apartment complex, and since I did not have any money to pitch for weed and I was always there to mooch off of them, pretty soon I wasn't welcome. They never told it to me directly with words, but I could feel it. In a way I did not care, or I did but I preferred to get high.

That year was the year I said I went from "Hero to Zero". I say it is the worst in my life because even though the consecutive years were worse objectively, that year is where I really felt the transition from taking drugs but having fun and life being good, to entering the real darkness, having people look at you and treat you differently and everything just come crashing down. All this was a nightmare for me because I lived to be liked by people, and the exact opposite was happening. What did I do? I ran away. On summer vacation I went to Mexico to visit my dad and his wife in and I did not come back. Thinking that everything was going to get better. I, however, did not realise at the time I was bringing all the inner trash and bad vibes, behavioral, addictions with me.

I had started to party with my stepbrother. Repeating patterns reproduced the same effect everything went to shit. I started smoking and doing LSD and ecstasy at parties in the open, and it is way more taboo in Mexico than in the states. I became known as the town junkie. I developed a horrible reputation.

One night while we were on our way to a rave, a voice inside of me kept saying "don't go…. don't go… you will regret this for the rest of your life." I did not pay attention and I went anyways. I took 6 LSD hits. LSD makes you want to pop your back. I was there in the crowd popping my back and I felt something that I had never felt before nor have never felt again. As I was moving my shoulders towards my back and arching my back to pop it, instead of feeling a pop sensation, I felt my spine evaporate. Like it disappeared into thin air. It scared me because I had never felt that in my life. When we get home, more than fifteen hours had passed, and the effects had not worn down. Two days had passed, and I was still seeing the LSD visuals. Four days passed and they were still there. To this day I still have LSD visuals. They have gone down, and I do not feel like I am tripping, but they are there. Sometimes I forget they are there because it's so minute, but I can feel in the darkness, that they are there. I do not know if they will ever go away.

Enter stage 4. Constant emotional torment. I go back the United States to live with my mom and enter an outpatient rehab center. But every second for me is a living hell because I am only living in the past, remembering all the things that I have done, every five seconds and feeling disgust, shame, guilt, self-condemnation, remorse, and regret. It was like grabbing a whip and whipping myself emotionally every five seconds. More time passes. I get used to being and getting high alone. When you are living in a state that your vibe, your energy is so low, that you are drowning yourself in your own hate and self-disgust, nobody wants to be near you.

There I enter my 5th stage. Kill Yourself.

Due to the constant torment that has now been going on for about two years or more, I develop an impulse, a reaction to it. First, I start saying "smoke weed" out loud every time I remember something that causes emotional pain. I say it automatically out loud without thinking. Like if I was some action figure that every time someone pressed my button. I would say my signature phrase. Later I realised it was my unconscious mind wanting to protect me from pain. That started to happen at the beginning of 2013 and lasted till I got clean in mid-2016. 3 years and a half of saying KILL YOURSELF every five seconds, sometimes every second, this painful loneliness, which was most of the time, was constant torture.

During this time was the second occasion that I declared to the universe "I DON'T CARE!!" It is interesting that the first time, two days later I got offered heroin, this time the next day I got offered crystal meth. It's like telling the universe, give me your worst! Because only after doing that I attracted these people who offered me the worst of the worst.

About two months later I was admitted into a rehab clinic. This was in August 2013, I lasted 9 months clean. It was not enough to notice any real change in me. Change starts to happen when you have a little more than a year clean, so I was almost there to getting a dose of peace, but I did not. I moved to Mexico City to study music production at a world, renowned school called SAE (School of Audio Engineering). That same day that I arrived, I relapsed. This was in May 2014. And so again I stepped into hell. Not even realising that I had stepped out for 9 months, until I stepped back in.

And so, my journey coming out of darkness begins.

By surrendering I was finally free. It was not until later in my personal reflecting I realised what I had experienced was rebirth.

My first year was the hardest. "If I could define my thoughts expressing them in words" it would be more like I was allergic to emotions. Anything, everything I felt caused me to react in a way I could not control. Sometimes I would have rage come out of nowhere, melancholy, fear. It was like I was emotionally stunted. It was a constant roller coaster of neurosis and insanity, and the way I was able to have the strength to get through it was going to meetings every single day releasing my emotions. Most of the time I would scream at the meetings, a lot of the times I would cuss out my workmates, support meetings were my salvation that first year. Being blessed to have an outlet a haven of acceptance to release in every day.

When I had about six months of sobriety back in the world after my time in rehabilitation, a total of nine months clean I had a sudden realisation that has impacted me to this day. "I know what my ultimate problem is, the reason I suffer. IT'S THINKING! Every time I think the thought process either has to do with the past, or the future, these constant thoughts are mainly unpleasant thoughts that link to pain. So, what is my main goal from here on out, to stop thinking." This allows me to accept the things I cannot change providing me the wisdom to understand the difference.

To this day I am constantly practicing mindfulness, being aware of my thoughts and catching them as soon as they pop up and letting them go. I started to realise the less I thought, the happier I was. That is why I loved smoking weed and its effects. I already loved to think, weed would explode that thinking to tenfold. When I was using drugs and trying to stop. I would try to think my way out of the situation into the solution. It was only now I had comprehension of the solution. This was to stop thinking all together. I began to have the awareness that the more I thought when I was actively addicted, the worse my situation got. So same thing when I was in rehabilitation. I was trying to think my way out of it, trying to get to a solution.

My first anniversary arrived. July 21st, 2017. One year clean. Around 20 family members came to celebrate. It was like I had graduated college or something, to me it was nothing that special because now I was simply doing what I always should have been doing, but since I took my family through hell for a lot of years, they were almost happier than me it seemed. My mom rented a house an Air B&B where we had our family get together. The whole thing was dedicated to me, each person (cousins, aunts, uncles, close friends) took some time to share some loving words.

As my recovery continued, I noticed that the more things started to happen, my self-inflicted emotional torment ceased. I was not constantly living in the past and flagellating myself anymore. The "kill yourself" impulse ceased. Suddenly, I started to step into a place of peace, mentally, emotionally! For the first time in my life, I started really feeling peace... and believe me once you get a dose of that, there is nothing you want more.

My next personal experience called the "fourth and fifth steps" is where I found out that I lived to be liked by other people. I remember as a teenager I was always interested in sales, I always wanted to have the courage to walk up to a random person on the street and start prospecting, selling them something. That point in my recovery eventually came. I was confident enough in myself to start selling. I learned to bake bread and started selling it in the Centro of Tequisquiapan. Averaging a sale of more than 100 muffins a day. I would wake up early, bake for about eight to ten hours, and then spend the rest of the day selling them. I would finish around 10 PM, and then repeat. I thought to myself, you have come a long way in your success from doing nothing except smoking weed and watching TV all day.

It was then that I noticed that everything that had been happening to me was part of God's plan. All realisations, my breakthroughs, my moments of transcendence, would happen when I least expected them to. That is when I really understood, felt, and knew, that God had my back. That is when I truly understood the essence of the third step. "We made a decision to turn our will and our lives over to the care of God as we understood him."

From that moment I started having real faith. Being open minded to whatever I need to transcend, when God decides it's my time, I put in my part and keep working on myself. Real faith that God has your back, that everything is going to be all right, that you are protected, you are guided, and while you follow the guide of God, what can go wrong? Right there something sparked inside me, a realisation, that it was time to bring and share my experience and knowledge and healing to more people, not just at meetings. It's time to scale up. Maybe I should write a book, put it into some rap tracks or something.

Life is telling me to go to record music. So that is when I decided and realised that my time in Tequisquiapan had come to an end. My phase of recovery, healing, and transcendence here in Tequisquiapan has wrapped up, I have graduated with honours. Mission accomplished. I started to sell some bread like before to have some money so that I can record songs. Each song is going to cost me ten thousand pesos.

It is during this time that I am selling in the "Centro" center of the town, that I meet Tracey Pagana. One thing leads to another and she asks me to write my story so she can fit it into her chapter in the book. In the past I had the realisation that it was time to share my story and knowledge on a bigger scale? Maybe write a book? Maybe telling my story in songs? In the same week, life called me to do so, both in song and in a book. I am blown away. When I think about it, it was the Trinity of Spirit that brought this together for me through people and connection. I heard God speak to my heart, and I said YES.

Life is becoming more and more magical and I could not be more grateful.

May you find peace and happiness.

God Bless

Marco

To think that the purchase of two cupcakes, a friendly smile, brought the union of two people connecting in the center of the middle of a small town nestled in the middle of Mexican Mountain is magical, wouldn't you all agree? The wonders that can happen, when Spirit connects with Spirit, his brave story in his chapter that brings a huge message, of love, courage, and sacrifice, as he attempts to shed light on a very dark subject matter that infects us all. Addiction.

There is nothing more I could add to Marco story his honesty, truth, his bravery, many times had me holding my breath and brought me to tears. Marco's sharing the choices he made openly touching on the deepest darkness moments of his living, teaches us all courage, through that darkness he kept one foot in front of the other. In the end, Marco was able to surrender all that darkness that kept knocking on the door of his heart. Marco gave his darkness over eventually knowing he needed a source much bigger than he to join forces to fight his way through the veil that had consumed him. This Veil consumed him but allowed him the ability to reach for his salvation and the light. He received hands on experience entwining, twisting, and his brokenness for over a decade living with incrusted dark energy seeping into every crack of his addicted body, mind, and soul.

The courage it took for this young man to dig out of that pit of despair and rise above to find the pinpricks of light he had lost sight of for so long was insurmountable. He is a real modern-day hero. My gut feeling is that never again in his lifetime will Marco experience going from hero to zero.

Your destiny, your courageous legacy, the hero you discovered inside your core is here to stay. I know his message of raw honesty will teach youth and young people all over the world addressing their pain. Marco's story will provide freedom, also by example the price some pay to find it. I also believe his faith and his love for the power he found connecting within Divine Spirit will infect the world in a different way, with the combination of Spirit filled energy he will invest his own self-love setting examples.

Marco you will make a difference for many because you stopped, invested the time, the energy, it took to make a difference for yourself. You Marco, did the work, your example will lead many to the light. It has been nothing short of a privileged honour meeting you. I want to thank you for having the courage to share your story with all of us. May you go in love, may you go in light, may you in all ways feel blessed, and may peace always reign in your soul.   May the true peace of Divine Spirit always be felt in the middle of your heart, bringing that beautiful smile to your lips. You are truly a real living angel who deeply marked my soul, Marco you will always have a haven of love a space inside the core of my heart.

RETURNING TO THE LIGHT

Its 6:45 AM I can smell the coffee brewing and think, "I am the luckiest person on the planet." Life is good and as I reflect on the experiences and had over the last six weeks here, I cannot help but feel a floodgate of emotions. Something about the warmth of the sun, awakening the morning as it rises slowly to start another new day. I think to myself to make it as glorious as the other days I have had over this precious time here.

I titled this chapter returning to the light for a few reasons. I wanted to address some of the emotions I am feeling while they are still fresh in my mind, now that I have my first cup of coffee in my hand, feeling the sun rising into the morning sky I can try to find the words to express them.

I have a bit of a melancholy feeling that is setting into my core. I have three more days and then this sanctuary of peace, calm, quiet will change for me. I will be heading back home to Ontario. It is not that I do not want to go home, I miss Joe and my clients, my friends, and the routine home life provides me at home. Here in this space, place, the quiet innocence, it provided me gave me the chance to heal. Healing to this level of finding pieces I never even knew where inside me. This emotion, the melancholy of it reminds me of the reverence silence has for me. The gift it provided me will remind me to step out when the noise or the demands get too loud when I return home. This emotion that I am feeling as I am trying to write, will remind me that no matter what is happening in my life on my return I can always very quietly close my eyes and bring myself back to this space, in my heart, in my mind and remember the feelings the experience of catching the light into my core, those healing rays of light, came shining through the glass with the morning sun. This light, this promise of a new day waking all the life that surrounds me will comfort me, warm my soul.

The gift of loneliness, living here in mostly solitude was at first extremely uncomfortable, to be honest after the first four days Joe went home. I truly wanted to ask him, maybe even beg him a little, to change my flight to come home. In fact, I think I even asked him once on a phone call if he would be able to change the date as I was having second thoughts. The ticket was not refundable, so it was not an option without a huge expense. I mentioned it was uncomfortable, but had a deeper desire to settle in, settle down.

I think sometimes the darker energy in life, the crippling self-doubt of change, the changes in the comfort of a routine that can keep a person in a space of simplicity, structure, is exactly what lower frequency wants from me. This frequency does not want growth for me it wants to keep me buried in a place where there is no self-growth. This energy wants to preoccupy my thoughts, my chores, and my life. We, as a society know that the speed of life has tripled since my generation 50 years ago. We did not have the technology like we do now. The good news about this is that I was able to see Joe and talk to him on my phone. This was a gift that provided contact and communication although we were careful not overuse the gift, again respecting each other's space and the work he had and I had to do, it was a gift. Still, routine was involved first thing in the morning and usually touching base with each other at night. Routine is something we are bound to as human beings. Routine teaches us structure, habitual things like morning coffee, walking into town the same way every day, favorite coffee shops, subject matters to discuss, food to eat. Routine is important, routine builds our foundation, teaching us to recognize, respecting the same foundation in others. My point, sometimes the lower frequency darker energy likes it when we stay submersed in routine. This energy collaborates with the speed of life, keeping us stagnated so we do not break out and learn to respect life differently, have fun, rejoice in love and play in the light. Remember the light is where we originated, when we agreed to come here, learn what we need to learn to help us transition to a higher respect for all life. What I really wanted to bring to the light in this paragraph is that it's hard, so very difficult to break routine for anyone and I honestly know this because for the first ten days of here alone all I really wanted to do was run straight back home into the craziness of my life. I wanted the noise of it to drown out my insecurities, the loneliness, that was starting to awaken in me in the silence of my situation. I felt trapped, scared, and completely confused in this silence. However, I knew this book had to be written, I knew if I stayed strong and open the wisdom would come and I would start to hear my own soul's voice. This voice leading me back into the light my birthright the safe, haven I was birthed from.

Insecurities, the quiet that brings them out from the depth of you are uncomfortable to face. It's comparable to a splinter you might get. It hurts initially when you get a splinter an object that is foreign to your body hurts and the first thing you want to do is grab the nearest set of tweezers and pull it out. So, what do you do? You pull it out, and you think you got it all, visually you cannot see the piece that is buried deeper. So, you get rid of the piece you pull out put, your brain may tell you to treat it with an antibiotic if it was a bigger invasion or use a band aid. You forget about it and carry on with your day. But what you may not realize is deeper in the wound there is a piece you were not able to pull out. This piece stays there until your body starts to work the stranger that does not belong in you out of your body. Energy that is not healthy for you works much the same way, but instead of your body working it out in the flesh your soul works this dark energy out with your Spirit. Both examples I have presented to you in this chapter take time. Time to fester, infect, and then reject bringing your whole essence back to a healthy state in your body and your soul. Insecurities surface when you have quiet time and you are not preoccupied with the noise around you. You even start second, even third guessing yourself. You may feel you need to spend some time reaching out to the people that mean the most to you. These people who are your team, your coworkers, your source of love, the love that validates your worth as a person. The people that make you feel like you make a difference in the world, their world. That is what happened to me in all this quiet time. I felt detached from my routine, the life I left, the team members I have, the people I talked to most days. The darker energy rose just like the fester from inside me, nagging at me, pestering me, reminding me I was not enough and needed that validation from others to feel secure and needed. It took a few weeks to settle in and not have to need that daily contact with people. It took me a few days to understand that just because my routine had drastically been altered, the routine in all the other people I love in my life had not. They carried on in their busy lives doing what their lives were calling them to do. I was the one who was in a state of stagnant, defining quiet. I was the one who needed to except this and deal with whatever the pain was causing me. In this case to reach out for validation and confirmation I was needed. This was my lesson to learn. Boundaries again here they were again. Always for me, boundaries, and listening I repeat these lessons over, and over again.

Just when you think you might have learned something valuable, and trust me in truth you have, I am reminded in the lesson there is another just behind this one that will teach me adding on to the lesson just received. Just poured myself my second cup of coffee into this chapter and wanted to say even more to myself than you, my beautiful connections who are reading this. I am more aware than ever of my expectations. I have come to terms with understanding, forming sustenance, adapting to the new habits I have adhered to in the past six weeks.

I wanted to talk about nutrition, the way I have been respecting my body differently. Of course, without Joe with me I have been eating differently. Joe and I are both emotional eaters, we tend to carry the stresses of the day out on the way we both eat, snack, we both just love food. It is a social thing for the two of us. It does not help matters that Joe can make anything he touches look like a five-star chef is serving it, and it tastes as good as its presented. The kids and I all love it when Joe is in the kitchen, he cooks, and serves his food with love, making all the difference in the world. It has made it easier with me here away from him to really listen to what my body is needing for nourishment. I start my day with a small bowl of healthy breakfast, hydrating more than I ever have, and eat small meals of mostly vegetable and protein throughout the day avoiding sugar, or having very little. I listen if my body wants a chocolate donut because I have walked for some time and it needs some instant sugar,

I find one that has been made fresh and not processed. I have been listening to my body and how it reacts after a piece of processed bread versus a piece of bread without preservatives. These changes are simple and consciously important for me to listen to. I also listen and feel when my body needs to have nourishment, not always a food substance. This is interesting, if I have been writing for hours my body says time to get up go out for a walk, get some fresh air, move your body, interact with people. I used to be caught up in how bad I looked in my clothes, how many wrinkles and rolls had developed on my body over time. I would feel disgusted when I caught a glimpse of my double chin, or the extra layer of fat I was tucking into my jeans to hide away from sight. Being here, listening to my body, my temple with a whole new love and respect for it has changed my perspective and new habits are forming. I know when I go home, I will not lose this perspective, nor the gift my body, my temple, the vehicle it provides the house for my soul. I have no intention of ever stepping on a scale again, using the words weight loss, as in, "this is how many pounds I have lost", or the word diet. I will promise myself to always listen to the needs, wants, desires of what my body is craving, asking me for, even in a social gathering. I will listen to the needs, and the desires my body, is calls me to whole health. I know, this was a long chapter, but truly feel it's warranted. I know that many people get caught up with changing their bodies by overindulging, it's easier to fill the ache, holes, that we all feel, when we are overworked, crunched for time, or just stressed. Momentum fuels this crazy speed, adding responsibilities life presents in our every growing world. Slow down, value what you are doing, how you are doing it, and listen to your body. It has a story to tell you.

Return to your birth, the Spirit you were born with, the one who knows you better than you know yourself, the quiet loving essence you committed to, joined forces with. Allow the natural flow of you, the rhythm of your life, the gentle voices calling you from within your whole essence, to embrace all that is healthy, strong, and good for you. Allow this growth, in the privacy of your own silence, teach you with a new perspective, the value of who you are, and what you can bring to the world and your own truth. Discover this truth in your self-discovery like I have.

Lastly this brings me full circle to expectations. Expectancy encompasses a need to resurface, revisits you time and time again as you progress in your life your journey of discovery and self-discovery. Expectations are varied, arise in all situations, especially when you are aware of your living with flesh, combining living Spirit. The sooner you reign in this emotion, agree to come to terms with the lesson that all expectations teach you. The sooner you will be able to tame the beast. As I have mentioned several times in this book as it was written on the premise of addressing darkness, and the effects dark energy, darkness, will always be one of your biggest teachers of all time. Without this energy we would not be able to understand what it takes to shed it, learn from it, release it. Never reject the messages dark energy teaches. However, we do not need to stay in the clutches of despair, surrounded by its company in the throes of its darkness. We can, and will, rise to the light! Stop expecting anything is going to change, you will still have hardships, loneliness, and personal battles. You will still suffer loss of life to the people who are taken before your time. You will still suffer grief, financial hardships, addictions, recovery! Living life in honesty and truth does not promise anyone a "fairy tale" ending. Life, the reality of living proving a ton of ups and downs. However, there is secret, to accepting it, the formula, is simple. Live fully in your freedom of acceptance in all your expectations! You then, simplify the learning you needed, resulting peace, in the closure of the lessons that provided peace.

Peace, true internal peace, is like that little piece of festering infection it eventually rises to the surface forcing its way out of the hole that pierced it initially. When it comes out with all the poisons, revealing, exposing itself, releasing out of the opening, it never returns. You heal, and you find restoration in the new growth that is happening in the space it was lodged in. Peace reigns and it grows redefining you, encouraging you. Peace changes your perspective allows you time out and teaches you to love deeper than you ever dreamed possible. Peace allows you to listen and accept without expecting change. I am ready in some ways to go home, the same person but with different tools in my toolbox. I know going back to all that noise and all the demands of the world I came from that may not change but, I know that I have had an awakening, a shift of self-discovery. I pray with all my heart I can help bring more gifts to the people seeking knowledge within themselves. I will do my very best to commit to the cause, respect, and love I have for Divine light. I pledge my soul, helping as many as Divine Spirit sends. I am grateful for all of you who share this journey with me as we, inject the world within us, around us, with the power and the healing while light energy provides for us. My desire for all, is that you find the strength within your own calling to rise, up, defining all the darkness that may encompass you. I pray that you find your courage to rediscover your own white light, internal torch, you deserve the gift of reconnection it's your birthright, your Divine destiny!

As always, in all ways I love you, carry you in my heart space, wishing each and everyone one of you

White light and love,

Tracey

Part Two

Passages from Darkness to Light

DEFINING DARKNESS

How many of you feel completely uncomfortable in darkness? If we are all being honest, I would wager a bet a fair number of you reading this book struggle with the uncomfortable foreboding darkness presents; yet we need darkness for many reasons. Darkness gives our bodies a chance to rest and recover from the routine and activity light encourages. I have always been uncomfortable in dark places. For many years, even now as a grown woman, I find it hard to sleep without some form of night light shining not too far away from where I lay my head to rest. It is not just the darkness; it is what my imagination conjures up in that darkness that can get me thinking all kinds of crazy thoughts.

Can you relate to this? Darkness leaves me feeling uncomfortable, fearful, and sometimes even anxious. Darkness happens and when it does it brings out thoughts and actions that are not always of a loving nature. I am aware that darkness separates me from a place of warmth and comfort. When I am anxious in this darkness, I most often have dark thoughts. Of course, I try my best not to address the thoughts by keeping my mind busy or avoiding the state of darkness. I am fully aware that if I do not learn to address what I need to address, by avoiding the darkness I will always stay in the darkness, keeping me from the light.

Let me try to elaborate, explaining to you how I came to understand facing the dark places in the choices I have made. When you make a decision resulting in any kind of meaningful action, there are always repercussions or consequences. When you choose from a place of love and sacrifice you rise from a place of love and light. There is no residual guilt or remorse. You just make the right choice and continue your life, leading you to the peace you do not even know consciously you are working towards. If you make a choice that inflicts pain due to a selfish act, those actions can tend to come back and amplify, keeping you frozen in darkness, leaving little wiggle room. Dark energy feeds this action creating a place of stifling, uncomfortable energy within you.

For me, darkness is something I ran from, dodged, and avoided it for many years. I was never comfortable in its presence and still am not. Darkness has haunted me, advised me and corrected me. Darkness has been one of my greatest teachers.

I have been writing since the very early day, and, for the most part, I sat in the silence of the darkness. Outside this space I am writing in, I am surrounded by windows from ceiling to floor. It was very dark as the morning started to wake up, almost eerily quiet. I had chills all over me as I was writing this chapter, not from cold air, but from the presence of dark energy. As the perfect morning sun rose, it was so bright that I had to reposition my laptop so I could see the words I was typing. Even the thought of the sun and the promise of light brings makes me warmer. The light that appeared was already warming my bones and shining promise on the still sleeping day. In some strange way, this made me ache for the light in a way I had never been aware of or considered. It occurred to me that I take so many things for granted, like the gift of light as it unfolds like clockwork at the dawn of a new day.

Every day, we witness many beautiful moments of light versus darkness.

The deeper meaning of darkness, as in dark spots on my soul, has been a subject I avoided for years. I have made some very deep, dark choices in my life. This might be why I have kept myself so busy, so pre-occupied. I tend to skirt around the deeper, darker parts of me that I was not consciously mature enough to address for many years. Yes, we can all blame our circumstances or upbringing and how we were dealt the hand we were dealt by virtue of our birth. Many people do just that. Many people seek years of therapy to deal with their demons or stay so busy they bury the darkness so deeply they do not even know where to begin to dig it up and address it.

Defining my own darkness has been my own personal journey. It has been a pain-filled, deeply personal experience. I have hurt many people in my life; some very close to me and some are my own flesh and blood. I have made many selfish choices and worked through the very bone marrow and brokenness of the results of those choices. Defining darkness for me has been an ongoing way of addressing the mistakes I have made, becoming accountable for them, rising above the darkness, and finding the light in every choice I have made. Whenever I hurt someone, it feels heavy and soiled, and immediately presents the awareness of the darkness existing within me. I feel it seeping into my thoughts and my reaction to those thoughts. Sometimes, those hurts have backed me into a corner, allowing me to wallow in a state of silence as a guarded victim, licking my wounds and plotting my revenge. The darkness of those actions did serve a purpose, however; those actions gave me permission to avoid the truth, to stay in the darkness. Had I made a different choice; the light might have set me free sooner.

All these choices that have led me to this moment of awareness have given me fuel to ignite a position of less resistance. Defining darkness needs to be a very personal trek through dark woods and unsafe internal territory. Defining darkness takes courage and a big walking stick. Defining darkness is not for someone who does not want to grow or for a person who needs the comfort of complacency. Defining darkness is not an easy subject matter, even to have an open discussion about. Confronting the dark spots on your soul may be more personal than the best relationship you have ever had. Defining darkness, your darkness, is a very intense, face-to-face in the mirror, heart-to-heart, soul-to-soul, honest discussion about your life, the choices you have made, and the means to work through the darkness in those life experiences.

I will give you an example of one of the biggest gifts I ever received addressing a moment of darkness. I need to go back a few years, so please bear with me as I share this part of my life with you. I feel compelled to share this part of my journey, so you understand the gift.

Several years ago, in a past life within this one, I met a truly Spirit-filled lady. I always thought she was full of grace and I felt she had a special bond with Spirit. This lady had recently lost her sister to cancer, and we were directed separately by Spirit to take a course in our parish called Abundant Life. This course stretched over six weeks, but lead to several years of deep, connected friendship. Sometime later a second person, joined our Trinity of deeply connected souls, with none of us knowing where it would lead. We spent a significant amount of time together sorting out and sharing life. We had a strong connection and talked for hours at a time on deep subjects of the heart, cementing a trust in each other on many levels.

We all grew together. I now know, looking back in time, these friends were my biggest teachers and advisors, and I also know deeply that the lessons I have learned from these two women helped to mold me into the person I am today. Without going into all the details, I wish to share my pain, defining my moment of personal darkness, and my lesson learned through that pain.

Over the past three years, around the time I was writing my first book, I started to grow apart from the relationship with these women. I chose to dedicate my time, my life, to my partner and my calling and the connection I felt pulled to. Feeling something akin to agony as a result of my growing apart from one friend, I confided in the other and she helped me reach a decision that I needed to make, to sever the friendship and explore what I needed to dedicate my time and energy to. She was a pillar of strength, helping me dissect the truth of my situation and choosing what I needed to focus on at that point in my life. The only thing I regret to this day is that I did not have the courage to be honest with the friend from whom I was pulling away. Over time, another lady joined the group, and I continued to meet with them from time to time; however, far less frequently than before.

In December 2018, the person we all thought was invincible, the person who always turned the impossible into reality, the person who directed and manifested for all of us received some shocking news. She was three shifts away from retiring and joining her husband on their journey they had worked their whole life to achieve. She was diagnosed with stage four cancer! I learned of this devastating news at a dinner with friends. I said "pardon" a few times as I was trying to swallow my food and not faint at the dinner table. I excused myself and made three phone calls, one after the other, to these friends from whom I had distanced myself. Each one answered the phone call. I went home and tried to wrap my brain around what I had heard, how it had happened, the prognosis, and the course of action.

The next three months were a blur. I spoke to my friend occasionally and offered what I could to help her but was very careful about respecting her. She was angry at the Source I am committed to working with. She felt betrayed and cheated, as He had, in her heart, made her a promise and not delivered it. This made it a very sensitive situation, and I was having my own battle of the heart with that same Source, to be honest. I tried to reach out to the other two friends to see if I could get updates on her condition, and this is where I gained my biggest lesson.

I remember the phone call like it was yesterday. The voice was angry; volcanic, spewing venom angry. She asked me how I dared use her to gain information and who was I to use her like that. In fact, who was I to use her all the years prior and set conditions on our friendship by making myself unavailable during certain hours to allow me to focus on my new relationship. She accused me of reaching out only when I was in need, never considering that she waited for me to call when it was convenient for me. Her anger intensified to the point that she accused me of believing I was God and further stated I had pronounced I was God in my first book. I sat in a state of shock long after I hung up the phone, numb and barely breathing. What had I done? I felt like my heart had been shredded into a million pieces, and I had no idea how to fix it. She ended the conversation and the friendship that day. I have respected her wishes and not reached out; however, I felt very strongly that I needed to write about it in this chapter, Defining Darkness.

I took all her information and slowly digested all the facts she was brave enough to disclose. These were her truths, her thoughts; this was her experience of our relationship to unravel, not mine. But what she gave me was such a gift. She taught me the value of owning honesty, addressing my core values and my belief that I am God. Not that I believe I have the power of The Almighty. I do not. But that I am a piece of that living energy, connected as one Spiritual source. God lives within my being, and I believe we are all connected to God.

This experience taught me that I had used her goodness and held power over her by setting conditions on our friendship. How absolutely horrified I was when, in reflection, I realized in my ignorance that I had set boundaries of not being available to her without even discussing the situation with her. What a horrible, selfish person I created, getting everything I wanted in our relationship and not considering her needs. Truly a monster move on my part. And now, I was calling her to gain information, having her reiterate facts she did not want to discuss as she was truly grieving her own deep loss of her friend. I had made promises I could not live up to about lasting friendships and growing old together. This promise echoed in the silent pain of my heart. I had been holding on by a thread to the friendship, when, in fact, I had clearly already separated from them. That day turned into three or four months of digesting and forgiving myself for being so selfish towards a person who was grieving in her own way, trying to come to terms with her own deep loss.

I was lucky in some ways that the friend who left us taught us dignity in the few short months she had left to live. She went to visit her family; she spent time with her husband preparing the house for him to sell; she got busy being the incredible, no-nonsense, practical example of one of the bravest human beings one could ever be blessed to know. She left me this note dated February 28th, 2019:

"You only need to carry me in your heart, Trace. That's all I need."

I did not see her before she transitioned straight to Divine Light. I was not even at her funeral, which happened to be her birthday, April 3. I was on a flight to California invited to work with another light worker. I felt her though, soaring in the sky with the angels beside my plane; walking in the giant red woods, my feet in the earth beside an ancient tree, I heard her whisper my name. I feel her in every single healing session I participate in. I witness her light in the handmade, stained glass lamp she made me, as she cuts through the darkness with the promise to assist clients with her presence. And yet, there are still days when I slay the dragon of darkness trying to make sense of the hole in my heart. Defining darkness is something I have needed to recognize and battle daily. I can pierce the truth, reach for the light, shedding the darkness, reaching beyond what I ever imagined. Still, some days the darkness is heavier than I had hoped it would be. It is a constant battle; some days it is just harder to feel the light.

In conclusion, I truly want to thank my friend for being honest and loving me enough to teach me truth and accountability. I am grateful for forgiving myself in this lesson. This forgiveness has provided me the freedom to send her much love often. It has also taught me this great gift of never promising something I cannot deliver. Saying no, speaking that word and saying it with a complete and honest heart full of love and kindness may have very well been the biggest lesson I have learned in decades. Gratitude pours from a new well of hope internally, as I am still growing, grieving, and loving in Spirit the person we all lost in flesh. She was the humblest person. She taught us all so many valuable gifts. She will always live on, teaching us from a different space and perspective. I will honour and love her forever.

FEELING SPIRIT

I often inform clients in a session of healing that we all come from the source of loving energy. I tell my clients that Divine source is where they originated from, that we are born from source connecting Spirit to living flesh. In this combination of predestined journey, they experience the lessons this life provides them. We are born with all the components that bring us life including the energy from Spirit existence. Then, lessons I believe you had predetermined in some way before coming into this life, you now get to experience what you needed to and learning what you need to learn. By no means do I wish to imply I know all. I absolutely do not. I learn just like every other person does every day. I get to live in human form. I am only speaking from my own personal experience within my own way of finding, rediscovering, and claiming my own Spirit filled identity.

I was very young when I discovered I would feel or know things that others did not. Others in my home seemed unaware of how it made me feel fear and sadness at times. These emotions where all part of the empathic feelings I was experiencing during this time in my young life. During the early 1960's there was little understanding or knowledge of what the word Empath meant. There was little understanding of the emotional and physical responsibility that seemed to take over my young self. When you are little and feeling your own pain, also keenly aware of someone else's pain you are feeling, what you do not recognize, or identify, is that it can keep you in a place of complexity mixed with fear. In my circumstance it put me in a place where I often lashed out aggressively. I know there were times in my innocence and fear that my outbursts made a lot of work for my parents. They had their hands full, working cohesively trying to understand me, as they tried to gain control of my increasingly aggressive, behavior. Sometimes we all fight things we cannot identify or gain knowledge in.

Feeling energy at an early age brings you to places you never imagined possible as a child. It can also bring you to places of deep loneliness and sadness. Sometimes when our home was full of joy, happiness, harmony, I felt loved and cherished and deeply a part of things. Other times behind closed doors I felt the anger, jealously and fear. The secrets I knew of left me feeling the energy of these adult emotional true scenarios who were experiencing their own lessons in the same environment. When you are dialed into emotionally charged energy empathically, you are also subject to things that are absolutely none of your personal business. However, it does not stop you from feeling them and knowing things you should not by all rights be subject to knowing. It just means you are connected to the course, the source, of this energy. You are connected to the choice's others experience in the space you share together, in the teaching of their lessons.

Sharing space with my parents was often not easy for me. I was being taught to be responsible and learning respect is imperative if you are ever going to survive in this world. Respecting all life was literally beaten into us. I know I am not alone in this, as this was the way children use to be raised. This was a very rough phase of my childhood and a sad place to grow up in. When I felt the wrath of a hard slap, or the end of a belt, or a wooden spoon to keep me in line, it was very painful both physically and emotionally. I was always very inquisitive and very aggressive when poked. I had a very hard time forgiving that kind of discipline and quite often was surprised by the harshness of the punishment delivered. It is something I never got use to and never understood until I had children of my own. I do not ever recall a time I can say I really hurt my kids or delved out that form of physical punishment, however, in saying that I did punish my children with a different form of emotional absence. We all have our lessons to learn and develop.

Feeling Spirit at a very young age and not being able to identify what that feeling was, was very confusing to me as a child. I was seldom focussed. My mother deemed this lack of focus being self-absorbed and selfish. It hurt me deeply, causing deep scars. I did not share my things and I was jealous of all the attention my siblings received. I did not do well in school, as I could not concentrate on simple tasks. I lived in two worlds not understanding either one of them. I was often lost in class not able to grasp the concepts that the curriculum geared to teach me. I felt and heard the noise from both worlds and could not identify any place I fit in. I felt lost and very often, misunderstood. I was frustrated, exhausting all hope to be understood at any level. I was screaming from the inside out. I knew I was loved but I think it must have been very hard for my parents to like me. I had a hard time liking myself, fitting in and finding peace.

Darkness in the early years of life, when you are not yet old enough to put things together emotionally, can leave dark scars of doubt and fractures in a young sensitive child. In session we often go back the client, Divine spirt, me working as facilitator as we retrieve this child, "returning back" in time where they may have left their inner child behind. I reference this to a memory when the client felt victimized, by an action of another that they had no control in.

Feeling Spirit is something that you are born with when you come into human form created from the source you arrive intact, body, mind, Spirit. In a living essence you agreed to take a part of living in body form. Some advanced souls are aware of this connection as early as they become consciously aware even before they start to walk. Some never want to remember that source of existence feeling the Spirit flowing within. I believe it depends on how many times you have come to earth and live as human, how many lessons you want to learn, and how advanced you have become in the learning. We are given choices to learn, grow, and feel all the lessons we set out to learn.

Feeling Spirit teaches you that you have a responsibility to help others seeking the long road of defining light versus darkness. The road is filled with experience and connection. This connection of flesh and Spirit can be used as an internal and external compass, a guide, educational wisdom allowing you to feel the essence of your inheritance, mingled, sprinkled with stimulation providing growth both internally and externally from both worlds.

FORGIVING DARKNESS

One of the most profound memories as a child growing up in the Catholic faith was the season of Lent, and the story of the death and resurrection of Jesus. I remember feeling this dark shadow of pain on my heart when the season would approach. Being raised in a Catholic family, going to a Catholic school, and attending 8:45 AM. Mass every Sunday, we got used to the rituals this faith brought into our home. I do not, as an adult, practice this faith and all the rituals; however, I deeply respect what I was taught and where my roots have originated.

Shrove Tuesday, commonly called "Pancake Tuesday," is a traditional feast day at the beginning of Lent, with Ash Wednesday the following day. During the Lenten Season, individuals offer sacrifices and offerings of penance to in preparation to commemorate the Crucifixion of our Lord, Jesus Christ. This is followed by a rich ceremonial Mass on Easter Sunday, celebrating His Resurrection to life.

This time of the year always brought me deep sadness. As a child, I had a difficult time with the feelings that would gather and congeal in my heart. It hurt to hear how He was killed and the story that was told every year in the same way. I would often reflect on the words the Priest repeated year after year, as he repeated what Jesus had said. "Father forgive them, for they know not what they do." I find myself repeating those words today, in these times when the ignorance and selfishness of the world are at the forefront, clamouring to be noticed; in their passionate beliefs, cementing their ways to gain and grow in accumulated power.

Darkness represents power without thought, power that is thickly laden with conditional motives. Mainly, to gain personal gratification. Darkness is power that has a hidden agenda to control or conflict, with strong boundaries of injustice and greed. This dark, clouded power very subtly stops any reason to hold an open discussion hearing all sides of a situation. This power can build momentum and wants to destroy any form of weakness, kindness, or communication it feels may be considered a threat to losing its destructive momentum.

This power is fed by fear, greed, mass hysteria, and total lack of personal control. This power is closed minded, determined, and can feed and infect the hearts and minds of the some of the most intelligent human beings. It is so easy for any human being to take pain and insults personally. The threats and the intended hurt this power can bring is real. It can snuff out a life and feed like a wildfire in a forest, consuming all life and all good, living beings.

The Crucifixion of Christ is a prime example of what fear and mania can cause people to do. The fear of this dark energy exists in all of us. We are told in the story that the mob only grew in anger and conflict as the dark energy of harm and infliction roared louder. We strive as humans to battle these two forces fighting within us. It depends on who and what we are protecting; it depends on our deep life lessons and what those lessons teach us. It depends on how we were raised and how much damage and pain we have suffered. It comes from what colour we are, what race we belong to, and what we have been promised, taught, and programmed to believe in. It comes from our geographic place of birth and our surroundings, the comfort of wealth and prosperity versus the hard life of poverty. This fear can rise and fall and settle deeply into our brains, our hearts, and our souls. This fear causes actions we choose to live by, and to die by.

This fear can also teach us deep grace and gratitude that surpass all the lessons of lower frequency energy, giving way to the challenge and rising to address this fear with a different kind of living truth. This living truth is an action that is spreading worldwide. People are awakening to the Spirituality that is growing in vast ways around our cities, streets, and countries. This energy is louder and bolder and is opening people's communication skills. This results in less fear and an openness of acceptance.

I have noticed over the past couple of years the growing trend of awareness towards healing oils, crystals, and healing expos. People are tired of despair and chaos and are looking for ways to address the darkness that invades our news channels and headlines.

It is very difficult to want and need to forgive the dark energy that seeps into our cities, communities, countries, neighbourhoods, sowing fear and creating havoc. It takes dedicated, disciplined thoughts, like when Jesus said, "Father, forgive them, for they know not what they do." I catch myself often wanting to judge the injustices of the world and find myself falling into the trap of anger over the ignorance of those in power positions, saturated in selfish pride. Would I do any better, if given a position of authority and power? I would only pray that I would have a softened heart, remain humble, and listen.

Forgiving dark energy means you need to take a huge breath, a step back, and sometimes a step out of the heated injustices of mankind. It takes a kind heart, as well as understanding that people feeling threatened by a perceived loss of power tend to react in quick, reactionary self-protection. This often results in further desperate acts or disaster, even to the point of costing human lives. Desperation almost always leads to rash decision making, leading to further devastating outcomes.

Forgiveness, truly, is the only way to rise, heal, and climb out of this situation. This starts with always forgiving the ignorance in these scenarios that is agenda driven and violently emotional. Forgiveness, often mistaken as weakness, is a powerful agent acting like water on a brush fire. It quickly dissolves the heat, allowing you to get closer to the facts that need to be addressed, discussed, and resolved.

It was, and still is, hard for me to watch The Passion of Christ. Director Mel Gibson got as close as he could get without going back in time, presenting what it may have been like in those days and times, bearing witness to the Crucifixion. I know, for me, watching the scene where Mary, Mother of God was on her knees in that courtyard, knowing what was happening, trying to prepare herself for the outcome of her son's death, took my breath away. I mourned with her in her despair. Feeling her agony was physically constricting my breathing, breaking my heart. It sickened me, mortified me, and destroyed me. If I am being honest, as I was caught up in the passion of this incident, I did not know if I would have had the ability to forgive such cruelty. Being surrounded by the growing, cruel, dark power, I like to think I would have been brave enough not to get carried away with the crowds. I want to think I would have forgiven, even spoken up to that kind of cruelty. Even as I write, a deep understanding pools and gathers in my being of what Father Spirit is calling me to do: Rise above the pain, the suffering, the greed, the cruelty of mankind, to love the unlovable, the broken of the world and the unforgivable. As He states, we are His children, and every one of us deserves to rise out of the dark energy that holds us back from the pinpricks of light. We can see them always, even when we are surrounded by darkness. These lights are our guides, our angels, our hope, and our Spiritual connectors. These lights bring us redemption from and for ourselves, bringing hope and a chance to rediscover how we can best service our own true inheritances. We can reach for the light whenever we need to. These lights, no matter how small, have the power to pull us out of our darkness, bringing us fully into the light.

DARKNESS UNDERCOVER

Dark energy is the most subtle, sneaky energy that hides inside the shadows of our hearts, sometimes causing physical pain. Hence, the title of this chapter: Darkness Undercover. I want to explain how this energy tends to hide in places causing us to allow it to claim subliminal and destructive control.

I have experienced many repercussions from allowing this darkness to invade my space and saturate my world, my deeds, and my deep need for attention. I have allowed this energy to take over my entire life during dark periods, claiming my body and my thoughts. And all the while, I was not even aware of the trail of damage I was leaving in my wake as a result of my lack of responsibility.

When I married for the first time, in April 1976, I was under a veil of darkness. I remember knowing deep down that this was a very bad idea; however, I felt I had no other options and accepted my fate. I know now that had I been presented with options; I might have taken an entirely different direction. I felt trapped and sad. I felt broken, lost, and displaced. I was consumed with deep anger and resentment towards the man I married, which was devastating. To even attempt to write about this in such detail now brings up black sludge I will need to release and send it to the light after I write this chapter.

My husband and I were married longer than we should have been. It was not his fault or mine that we were brought together to experience our union. It was our choices that created the darkness we both continued to keep undercover. This darkness was hidden in our actions and lack of communication. We both were fighting for a spark of light that neither of us could identify, in ourselves or in each other. I was very broken, very immature, very self-absorbed, and very lost. He was very quiet, shy, brilliant, and focussed on his career. We never, ever, connected on a soul or ego level, all the while hiding in the world and putting on brave faces to try and build this life. Firstly, we had no idea how to find foundation in ourselves, let alone trying to raise our firstborn child, a beautiful son who was born to us on October 4, 1976.

We carried on under the veil of subliminal darkness, in denial that we had any problems. Of course, these problems and our failure to address them caused deeper emotional separation within our marriage. Without voice, our actions towards each other invited more darkness underneath the surface to spread and deepen the infection.

Shortly after the birth of our second child, a beautiful daughter born June 28, 1978, we realized that our small house in Southampton, Ontario, was not adequate for our growing family. We decided to purchase a larger home in Port Elgin. Something about that place bothered me deeply from the get-go. It was a fixer-upper, but my husband was quite handy and over time we adjusted, but the energy in that house was cold and unsettling. I distinctly remember a babysitter telling me she saw the face of a "mean man" who showed himself in a mirror, and she was so frightened she asked a friend to come and stay with her until we returned home. My daughter also told me when she was four years old that a man would appear to her, coming out of her closet pushing something, and he would go into our room and enter our closet. He never bothered her; she just would see him and tell me. I did not act on this information, but I can assure you, the hair on the back of my neck stood up as she told me these details. At the time, I was too Spiritually immature to address the situation, but I did find out years later that an elderly man who had had severe diabetes and had lost a leg due to his illness had passed away in our house. That would explain his restless wandering and possibly even his anger, as he may have chosen to cling to dark energy versus walking into the light.

There is a bright light moment in our broken union. While living in this house, my husband had an opportunity to be born again in Spirit and was invited to a weekend of healing through our church. The weekend was selective - husbands had to go first. My husband was picked up on a Thursday night, returning home on Sunday. When he arrived home, he was a changed man: kind, attentive, loving, and supportive. In all honesty, I did not know who the heck he was. It was very, very frightening that he wanted to be this loving, affectionate person he had not been for the entire five years of our marriage. This new person I was married to was someone I had never met. To be honest, I did not think I even wanted this kind of affection or a deeper connection with this person I barely liked and had never really loved. The darkness began to seep deeper into me, causing me to overeat while being glued to the television in between fulfilling my other responsibilities as a wife and mother. Supressing all this internal truth, it was just too complicated to deal with, and I slipped further into depression and did not deal with anything.

My retreat weekend was scheduled three weeks after my husband's experience. And so, my turn came. I remembered feeling extremely nervous about going to this potentially life-changing event. I felt unsure, unloved, and very vulnerable. I was picked up, as he had been, on Thursday evening, and returned on Sunday.

The experience was, in fact, life-changing in so many ways. I shed anger, disappointment and hurt. The veils were lifted from my eyes and, for the first time, I met my sweet Jesus face to face. (To this day, He is with me. I think we work well together!) I experienced a new birth that weekend. I felt loved and accepted by strangers at the seminar, and people I met that weekend continued to help me throughout the next few years, becoming teachers and guides for me. One woman was so motherly. She surrounded you with her huge heart and massive bear hugs so big you got lost in her embrace as she folded you in and gathered you to her bosom.

The weekend ended and when I arrived home to his warm embrace, I knew deeply that the damage was too great and the distance between us too far to ever recover. We managed to continue for a few more years, both of us trying hard. Too hard. It was unnatural. We never felt connected at the same time to form a healthy, natural bond. We just could never quite find our way to each other. Darkness undercover overtook our direction, clouding our view and halting our progress, causing deep canyons of hurt between us and eventually resulting in no way back for either of us. Dark energy is real. It can cause an unstable situation you can never recover from. For me, it led to the end of my first marriage. Of course, this is from my perspective only, reflecting my side of the experience.

I spent several years after we separated and divorced drowning in a pool of dark energy and bad choices, bringing a lot of dark energy into the lives of the people I loved, including my two incredibly amazing children. It took many years for me to realize the detrimental effects of this dark energy that had consumed me.

So, what changed?

Accountability is a life-saving device and one we all should consider. Taking responsibility for one's actions and the choices we make is liberating and fills our hearts and souls with healing light energy. I encourage everyone not only to grab the ring of knowledge, but also to accept fully and embrace the healing light energy provides. Become the person with the strength to forgive yourself, and then, with an honest, open heart, ask for forgiveness. This is the only true way I have been able to come out from under that thick curtain of suppressed, subliminal darkness undercover. Being accountable allows us the strength to make amends.

THE POWER OF SILENCE

It has taken me many years to find comfort in silence. When I was troubled and making choices out of desperation, it was even more taxing. Spending any amount of time alone only led to more spontaneity, resulting in - you guessed it – more bad choices. Silence left me in a restless state of anxiety and deep loneliness. Often, silence would sneak into my head, freezing out any good thoughts left there.

Silence in those years was something I avoided. You would never catch me reading a motivational book, going for meditative walks, doing yoga, having a massage. It was just something I never allowed myself to enjoy. Silence was always ominous; it hurt my heart. So, I ran from it, as far away as I could, never even once acknowledging its presence. The buried silence within was screaming at me to give it a chance to introduce itself to me. In fact, I was so petrified of silence that when my first husband worked the night shifts and left me in our home with our children, I would bundle them up and go to a girlfriend's for sleepovers so I did not have to be alone. To say I was terrified to the core of my being would be completely and utterly accurate.

What was I afraid of all those years?

When I was very young, I was afraid of all the Spirit noise I could hear but did not understand. I was afraid of the unspoken energy in my home. I was afraid of the kids at school who were bullies. I was afraid of saying the wrong thing, which happened often, and I was afraid of the consequences when I said the wrong things.

So, the silence I feared within me was always covered up by the noise I thought I needed. I often acted out in a loud way to be heard which would bolster my low self-esteem. I was always a passionate person, and, as far as I know, I was always driven. Underneath all that clutter was fear, misunderstanding, loneliness, all of which resulted in my having no direction.

The despair within me only grew bigger as my loss of control got wider. I was married very young and had responsibilities beyond my capability. I can say now that in those years there was something missing in me. I was disturbed and needed help. The silence only grew.

But Divine Spirit had a plan for me. In all that silence, Spirit was able to remain in a place deep within me, waiting for a time when I would reach out and commit to myself to choose His guidance. We all need to step out of self-saturation, so we can address our silence that gets crowded by noise.

Addressing your silence is not easy. It can be very painful to address all the bad and good parts of how you have conducted your life. In your silence, you cannot avoid all the horrible things you may have done or said to someone, how you may have reacted, how your decisions may have destroyed another human being or, perhaps, inflicted a pain so heavy they may still be healing from those scars. You need to be brave, strong, and confident when addressing the silence that may be buried layers and layers deeper than you were aware of. The power of silence is the biggest gift I ever allowed myself to receive.

Years ago, I attended a silent retreat and have written about it in my previous books. If I had had any forewarning of what was going to happen on this retreat, there is no way I would have signed up for it. I died at least three Spiritual deaths during this retreat, one death being so painful that my body curled up into the fetal position as layer upon layer of pain wracked my body. It took time to understand that my body was releasing toxins and scars, some of which may have been held through many lifetimes. At the time, however, I had zero knowledge or comprehension of what exactly was occurring inside me. I was so Spiritually immature at this retreat I had no idea of the deep respect that was required to be committed to the vow everyone took to be silent. I was constantly trying to make eye contact or communicate with a smile. I was sensing our guru, Sister Jean, was annoyed with my immaturity and tried her best to show me the message of silence through her loving patience. I was so eager to learn, fit in, and make a difference on my newly acquainted healing path. I was missing the point completely, but like a grasshopper grows, she took the time to demonstrate for that whole seven days the power and the disciplined silence. Eventually, on the last day, as I was sitting having my lunch on the grass of the grounds, I felt the wind coming across the space I was sitting in. The breeze, like the hand of Spirit itself, touched the grass like it was being caressed in love and respect. The breeze reached me and softly tickled my cheeks, my face, my whole body, leaving its mark on my head and running down my hair, my back as if to say in the most profound way, "In silence you will always know I am near."

The power in those moments of silence never left me. Even 20 years later, I can still remember every aspect of that day as clear as a bell. Sometimes, in the busy flow of life, I tend to leave the silence, but then I am reminded often how much I miss it. There is a power that grows deeply within you when you take the time to embrace your own personal silence. This silence shows you how to make peace within and how to find your truth, accountability, honesty, and awareness.

What was I afraid of all those years? I was afraid I could not ever be forgiven for my actions, my thoughts, my deeds, or my secrets. I was in deep shame for my actions that had caused people pain due to my selfishness and my pride. I was afraid no one would ever love such a damaged person. I had no idea how to even begin to truly love myself. The power of silence strangled me and kept me so busy I would not make one ounce of room within me to even attempt to address all the damage underneath. Then came my healing journey during the silent retreat with Sister Jean. At the retreat, I met a special woman who radiated love. She was a white-haired, living angel, and I later learned she was a Reiki Master. Honestly, I felt her energy silently speaking to my heart, asking me to rise out of my dark cloud and join her on a journey of sisterhood healing.

Is there darkness in silence? Yes, there truly is, especially if you have lived in pain and self-sabotaging energy in choosing how you will live your life. This lower frequency darkness feeds on the carnage, the leftovers, of your unresolved lessons. This energy keeps you in a place of low frequency and whispers in your ear, on your heart and in your soul that you are not good enough to be forgiven. It whispers, "It's too late! There is no way you can make a difference. There is no way you can reconcile any of your mistakes. You have made your bed, and now you must lie in it. There is no way back from the damage and destruction your choices have created."

I know this to be untrue! Trust me! I have broken many hearts and many promises, and I am very aware loving energy has taught me that by being honest, with yourself and with others, always in kindness, choosing to rise above, addressing all truth in your deepest silence, there is always forgiveness. First, by forgiving yourself, accepting and addressing what is yours, and asking for forgiveness, these actions of accountability educate you, supplying you with new tools to work with. These tools release you from the pits of darkness, where this dark energy constantly feasts off your misfortunes.

While living in Mexico during the writing of this book, I felt the acquaintance of silence deeper than I have ever been gifted. Yes, silence is a gift that was received fully in this sabbatical. However, it was very uncomfortable at times. I have a problem being in the darkness in this silence. I cannot see in the darkness like I see in the daylight. As the darkness fell around that space, it changed my security. It caused me to feel more vulnerable and more guarded. I felt the change as the darkness took over the light. The silence within had a voice, I had not, recognised before. This new voice that was rising with in me instilled a calmness over me. That new calm continued to keep growing the more time I spent with it. That calmness assured me darkness was present gifting awareness. That darkness represented had no intention of harming me and had no power to harm unless allowed in. That darkness was needed so that I could awake and rise from its shadows to embrace the light that will come, that always comes, filling my being with new promise, new lessons, and new hope. That light was healing and taught me to rise addressing adversities. It helped show the direction of the day, my purpose, hope, my dreams of a promise to love anyone and everyone in my path. I am living in a pattern of continual growth.

I want to share a secret. I still sleep with the bathroom light on when my sweet Joe is not snuggled up in bed beside me. I sleep hugging a pillow so I can feel an object of material comfort in the dark. I then invite my mother-in-law Betty who has transcended to Spirit almost four years now to snuggle up with me, I adored her. I sleep with the light on so I can identify the objects that leave shadows in the darkness.

I encourage you, truly I do, to take a day where you shut off all technology, all sources of noise that take you away from your own internal silence. I encourage you to sit in complete silence allowing time to experience your own internal gift of life. I encourage you to walk in silence, talk to yourself, in your own sense of your true self, listen to your private thoughts, and really listen with intention. I am not promising this will be easy. It will not be. You will be tempted to retreat, stepping back into the loud, crazy, fast-paced world we have all fallen victim to. I do promise you that it may very well be the most uncomfortable state you have ever given yourself permission to experience. I also know that you will, if you trust yourself enough, have a huge, enlightened awakening.

Allow this silence to help you reclaim the power you have not addressed, maybe ever. The power of silence is a gift yet to be opened, revealed, and secured in the centre of your being. Learn to respect the gift and the power that lives within you. It is in your grasp! You need only to step out of your safety zone and into the arms of the Spirit-filled silence awaiting you. Love yourself enough to spend a day in silence. Then you, too, will be able to feel the magic growing in this gift, as you define and align the gift of your unique being that holds your truth and reveals layers of your worth.

SHADOWS IN THE DARKNESS

Some of the chapters in this book have been challenging to write. Putting painful memories and emotions into words and sharing them with my readers has been very difficult. This chapter is no exception. Sometimes I think, if I could dig a big hole and bury these memories forever, I would do it. However, at some point, the shadows of past actions inevitably come to the surface, and we need to face them, address them, and then release them, so we can come to a place of acceptance within.

Addressing the dark choices of our past is never an easy feat, and I sigh deeply at the realization that we all have skeletons. Confronting these skeletons allows an acknowledgement of our past and reveals secrets tucked away in closets. Confronting these skeletons gives us permission to have a good airing out, clearing out, and creating new space for clarity and healing.

Shadows in the dark are the black sludge of poor choices that leaves residue in your mind that consciously collaborates with your ego. This clearing out invites an opportunity to heal scars from past decisions made from selfishness or anger.

To explain further, I will share some personal experiences I have had learning about these shadows.

Anyone who knows me would never believe I was a very mean-Spirited child. In truth, I was very unkind to my siblings, acting out with anger, judgment, and harsh behaviour, often hitting my siblings or hurling insults and names. Truly, I was not a nice little girl, often jealous of the attention shown to my siblings. I do not really know why I was so ignorant in so many ways; it was just a deep-seated resentment I felt that often showed up in my actions. I was not a person who was conscious of caring, even in my youth. It made me feel good to be mean; it gave me control through my tormenting actions of aggressive bullying. I am not proud of this. It was just the way I was growing up. If I was nice, to be honest, there was always an agenda behind the kindness. I chose myself first always and did not consider any other possibilities.

The way you live your life as a young person continues with you as an adolescent, and my selfish ways continued to follow me into my teenage years. I often stole candy, and then got brave and started to steal bigger objects, like clothing from department stores. What was disturbing as an adult was the fact that when I started to clean out this closet, metaphorically speaking, I felt no remorse at all for having done those things. I stuck it all away in my huge internal closet, reasoning that the store owners were richer than I and could afford the donation. It has been over 40 years since I committed these crimes, so the cobwebs are thick and nasty in this opening-up, revealing this hidden information publicly makes me feel sick to my stomach. The shadows of darkness in these very dark places allow me a chance to ask for forgiveness. Bringing this information out is literally like coming out of the closet, and it instills fear of judgment or persecution, as well as other thoughts that are surfacing from that dark place. My body is also reacting in a deep physical way. I am sighing deeply and grieving in the way you would when you are trying to accept your penance and practice self-forgiveness for your crimes.

This behavior carried on for me until my early thirties, and I was oblivious to the damage I was creating in my life or in the lives of others. In finally awakening to this destruction, I realized I had never addressed the issues or revealed the darkness lurking beneath the surface and exposing itself in habitual, destructive behaviour.

I had been too broken to look. It was too painful to address. I had been running on empty for years and had never considered there was another way of living. Everything I had ever truly loved had been taken from me, and I felt confused, depleted, lost, and exhausted. Shadows of darkness only grow bigger if you do not find a way to address them.

These shadows can and will eat away at you, slowly taking you in and swallowing you up until nothing remains. This darkness will stunt your internal and external growth. Had I not decided to turn my life in another direction and choose to dig deeply, to clean out, and to discover another solution, I would still be on that path of destruction, under the power of the shadow of darkness.

This all changed for me about 17 years ago, when, for the first time, I loved someone enough to choose to address the veil of darkness and lies we were living in. I will not go into the details of this relationship out of respect for the individual. I just knew if I were not truthful, I would not grow out of the shadows we had created.

This led to a sabbatical life for the next three years, when I worked at discovering who I really was. This time allowed me to rise out of the shadow of darkness that had consumed my entire life and to fully face my truth. Not only did I face it, but I also started to do the right thing. I decided to come from a place of full circle and honesty. My description for full circle is to access and address all your deeply buried secrets, acknowledge them, own them, dissect them, and, most importantly, understand the reasons for your choices. This can be painful. It takes strength to face all your shortcomings, but it also gives you the deepest understanding of yourself. In your discovery, you will be able to begin your personal path to self-forgiveness. In this process, combined with white light of compassionate Spirit energy, the shadows start to dissipate. All that is left is the information of your choices and the means and capacity to forgive others for their shortcomings. You are left with a great understanding of what humility means.

This is the most exciting news. When you break down your own walls on a quest for truth and self-discovery and can forgive yourself for the most heinous crimes, thoughts, or choices you made, no matter the reason, you get to know yourself in a whole new way that no one else can ever break. This wisdom and understanding create a strength you will no longer be able to deny yourself. This power teaches you that holding on to your darkest moments, the ones that left shadows of self-doubt, is no longer required. This power allows new light to enter your being, resulting in new internal growth and confidence that need no protection.

This knowledge means straight up freedom and this is a promise that I can make. Why? Because I live in this light every day. You will never live in personal fear of any kind that keeps you a prisoner to your past, hiding in shadows of your choices. When you can address your darkest moments, you will find the courage and the grace to forgive them with the help of loving energy. You need never fear them again. Yes, you will be scared and lost and lonely at times; that is just living and learning the lessons that come with being human. My promise is you will not live in fear because you have addressed all the secrets that hurt your heart and create a place of fear and deny yourself the light, life, and forgiveness you seek. The shadows had total control, and you were living in denial of your truth. There is far more power in Divine Spirit connection than any shadow darkness provides.

The truth is, we come from perfect Spirit. We come to learn and commit to learning. We come from a source that supports, us, teaches us, and loves us. No matter what we do, we can and will return home and reunite with this love, bringing with us all the information this life has presented to us. When you address all that pain in you, nothing else can ever hurt you! You will know how to rise above and come to an agreement within you that supports all you are, accepts all you are, and loves all you are. You, in your complete wholeness, can be that beacon of hope, for others still trapped in their dark shadows of pain. I believe in you, and I urge you to take the chance to also believe in yourself!

SLAYING DRAGONS BORN OF CONFRONTATION

Confrontation is something many of us try very hard to avoid. Some may even admit to avoiding it at all costs. It can cause irreparable harm and painful rifts between family, friends, husbands and wives, parents and children. I have had my fair share of confrontation in my life, sometimes causing huge holes in my heart, sometimes teaching me even bigger lessons of truth and boundaries. I want to share with you a few of these moments, how I acted or reacted, and what I learned in hopes that the information may be of some help you. Some of my personal examples of addressing the negative energy involved and the outcomes may also ring true in your own life.

When I think back to my childhood, I was very angry at my sisters, especially my middle sister. I was always jealous of her relationship with our father, and it was obvious to me that he favoured her. She was smart and could write and draw. She was a good student and always seemed to get the reaction from him I thought I should be getting. She did not even have to try; he just liked her. This caused me to be confrontational and mean to her; in fact, I used to threaten her relentlessly. I am embarrassed to even admit this, but I bullied her into stealing for me. Yes, I was a bully. As it turned out, she got caught by the store owner, which landed her in a whole heap of trouble with our mother. I do not think my sister ever told my parents I was the one who made her steal. But in saying this, I know she suffered the repercussions of her actions, and I know she was very embarrassed. This caused a lot of heated moments of confrontation between us in our bedroom. It also provided a wall of pain and did not do much to build a bond of sisterly love; in fact, it caused us to grow apart. I do not think she could ever trust that I had good intentions, even when I truly did. To be honest, I did not have good intentions, for the most part, in those years. I was a very nasty sister and very unkind most of the time. On many occasions, I chose darkness over being kind to my siblings.

Two things happened after that bullying incident. For one thing, I know for a fact she never tried to steal anything ever again. She was always a good girl, respecting the law, respecting life. Secondly, and this took me years, but when I asked her for forgiveness, she responded without having to even think about it.

Confrontational energy can take many different forms and develop from a vast spectrum of personal agendas covering any number of topics from the mundane to the catastrophic. It can cause disagreements that result in personal conflicts and dissolution of relationships on a personal level, and run the gamut to war, famine, embargos, and annihilation of human life in the extreme. The main ingredient to any confrontation, in my personal experience, has been passion regarding a difference of opinion or deep personal belief. Passion seems to fuel the debate, the conflict, and leads to confrontational exchanges.

Many years ago, someone very special to me felt called, at a very young age, to join the Jehovah's Witness. To be perfectly honest, I felt very uncomfortable with her decision and with this religious group for a long time. My friend tried to help me understand their beliefs and practices, and their vision of the future. She tried to explain the allure to me, and I tried with all my heart to understand it, but we agreed to disagree. What hurt me the most in this situation was the fact that she believed at the time that if I could not buy into her committing to this religion, I could not spend eternity with her. Many confrontational conversations took place between us, resulting in a deep chasm of silence. The subject was taken off the table, with no compromises of any kind. This faith-filled community became her new family support group for a time; however, she left the practice for a few years, and secretly, I was very happy about that decision. Still, we did not discuss the differences between us. Years later, she rejoined the practice, this time bringing her family into the fold.

This second time around was even more painful for me, as I was not allowed to ever recognize her birthday, Christmas, Easter, or any significant holidays. At first, I needed to stand my ground, and again with confrontational passion, to plead my case for Christianity and the celebration of holidays special to me. At the end of the day, all that is left is your truth, but your truth may not be the way someone else sees it. I had to swallow my pride, my strong belief, and allow another opening in my heart to accept the fact that she was happy raising her family connected to something she strongly believed in. I had to force myself to think outside my traditional Christian upbringing, accepting and respecting her beliefs and the way she wanted to raise her family. I am not going to lie. It was difficult adjusting and not slipping back into my old habits of celebrating special days and events and showing respect for her beliefs. Even though I will never understand the faith of her choice, I have learned to love her for what she loves, and to honour her belief with a quiet reverence.

This could have gone very badly, as confrontational, unresolved differences often do. Sometimes, we need to look at the bigger picture so we can still grow in our lives and accept and honour the choices others make although we do not agree with them. This does not mean we cannot still grow together in other ways, supporting each other with respect and dignity. Our dearest and closest family members and friends teach us lessons, often, through confrontation.

We all want to make a difference in this world, to leave our mark, to have a chance to say what we mean and mean what we say. The world is full of advice, opportunity, discovery, and we all have a seed of passion that is alive within us. We all, if given a chance, want more than anything to feel loved, valued, and accepted. Leaning to find your own way to fill this void will be your personal challenge. I encourage you to think before you react, to think through all the consequences, and to set an example of kindness and love in any confrontational situations, or you may very well find yourself either ankle deep or all the way up to your knees in quicksand. I can promise you if you take the time you need to work it out, think it out, and then ask for a little Divine encouragement, you will always find your best resolution.

I wanted to share something with you in this chapter that was difficult to share. This experience was very personal, but I felt it important to give you examples of confrontational exchanges I have had with the people I have loved and still love with all my heart. I wanted to teach you that no matter what happens or how far apart you are in your beliefs, you can always choose a different outcome to any and every situation. By playing nice with confrontation, it loses its power rather than gaining momentum and resulting in ultimate destruction and loss. It fizzles out and becomes peaceful. Peace reigns in a collaboration or compromise between two loving beings, with the power of grace and a sprinkle of mutual respect.

KNOWING LIGHT IN DARK DISAPPOINTMENTS

Disappointments are going to happen in your life. They are going to arise in relationships, work environments, and social engagements. There are different levels of emotional responses we suffer from when we are feeling disappointment. In my perception and my experience of being disappointed, it has always boiled down to what I was expecting and what did not manifest for me in my intentions or my desires.

About twenty years ago, I worked hard to find an original song, hire a musician to compile a melody for the song, pay for studio time to record the song, and submit the final product. I was sure the song was a hit, and I was bound to receive a Canadian Music Grant. I waited as my excitement was building and my dreams were already setting sights on being accepted and building my music career. Secretly, I saw myself at the Canadian New Artists Awards. The weeks went by, and my heart sunk deeper with each passing day. It was several weeks before the letter finally arrived. "Thank you for your submission." It was a very polite, generic, rejection letter.

What did I do? Well, I spent some time trying to not feel sorry for myself and carried on. You see, what happened next was Father Spirit's direction, for my music and eventual recording manifested into reality, not for me, however, this music was for healing broken Spirits. I have said this phrase often in my life: "When God shuts a door, He opens a window."

I remember it like it was yesterday, still so clearly etched in my mind although it was over twenty years ago. I was sitting in quiet contemplation on a tree stump in Alvinston, Ontario. The stump and natural habitat made for a pretty place, including a spring-fed pond surrounded by natural vegetation. The area is a conservation area, full of natural life. At the time, we had a trailer, and this was the view to be front of our lot. It was a majestic, peace-filled, silent environment. So silent in fact, it may have been the very first time I heard God's voice so distinctly. The voice that I heard in my heart was so loud that I turned my head around to see if someone was standing behind me. This voice was a strong, kind, firm, masculine voice, and He said, "Tracey, you are going to sing for me now." Imagine that! His voice, having no doubt of its origin, asking me to sing for Him.

I was not kind to the voice I was hearing. I let that voice know I was not interested in singing Spiritual music. I had my heart set on soft rock or country and had no interest in singing music related to Christianity, or God Source. I was cheeky, even a tad disrespectful; a selfish girl, as I recall the banter with my Creator. The voice stayed calm and said, "My child, one door will open another and you will sing for me. This is your path." I was a bit rattled, to say the least. I was still depressed and extremely disappointed my singing dreams had not manifested in the ways I had wanted.

About a month went by, and I started to forgive the music industry. I began thinking that maybe there was something deeper I needed to contemplate, and for the first time, I considered the voice I had heard. Through a chain of events, I was asked by a minister and his musical director to sing at one of their Sunday services. This was a new congregation in town called The Worldwide Church of God. The minister's name was George, and he was a very kind, Spirit-filled pastor. The music director was John. The three of us engaged in a conversation that led to discussion of the music grant. As I talked about it openly with these two gentlemen, my honesty seemed to intrigue them as I continued to share everything, even the message from the voice on the tree stump.

What happened next was absolutely, Divine intervention. John took me on, spending hundreds of hours recording, writing, and singing in his basement studio. He took the time to introduce me to a minister named Scott, who, after my testimonial, handed over five of his own personal songs so that I could record my version of his creations. Another individual named Todd shared with me his story of brokenness and how he found his Spiritual essence and gave me a song to record called *Face to Face*. The recording was released and went on its way of anointing and healing with the reverence and energy Spirit deserves. I could talk more about where it has travelled and how the resonance of the Spirit alive in the music has healed, but my point of this chapter is: out of a dark place of disappointment, not only did I find love, passion, compassion, and grace. I also realized on the deepest level, out of darkness and despair and disappointment, we are all being guided by a loving essence that not only knows what we need, but also wants to give those needs directly to us.

I witness all kinds of disappointments, where individuals grow in the lessons and actions that have happened to them. We can get caught up in the idea that life is not fair. Well, the truth is no one ever said it was going to be fair or easy. Things happen to people all the time: infliction, disease, accidents, death, sickness, poverty. Life is not always fair. Most of the time we do not understand the depth of another's suffering, the fate life has bestowed upon them. However, we can and should stand ready to stay open with our ears and our hearts, setting our own thoughts and opinions aside, making room to just listen from within our hearts.

The biggest lessons we learn are often taught by the people we love, the people we are invested in. They teach us healthy boundaries. Why? Because if they really love us, they will take the time and energy to teach us boundaries, helping us learn the truth about ourselves. I have been more disappointed by my family and close friends than any other more casual relationships. These individuals teach me where I fall short and where I excel as a person. The disappointments hurt so deeply that they force me to make healthy changes. Truth hurts, but the hurt makes me aware; the awareness spawns change; the change allows self-awareness, resulting in new birth and internal growth.

My children have taught me repeatedly that I cannot fix their brokenness. All they truly want is for someone to hear them. This means that I do not offer advice; I just listen. When your children hurt, you just want to fix their pain, but I have had to look a bit deeper and learning not to take on the pain they are feeling because of the disappointments their lessons are teaching them. When our children or anyone else we love are hurting we tend to want to fix their pain instead of labouring through it with them on the sidelines. I have figured out why I always want to be the fixer. If there is a solution I can offer, the pain diminishes, but the real reason is it also diminishes for me. This realization was a huge moment of awakening for me. If I could fix their pain, I no longer must feel their disappointment. I get to solve the problem, feel good about being the saviour, and move on to more living.

This has been a huge lesson for me and a humbling one. Listening, just listening. And yes, I do have to practice this daily. Anyone who knows me will smile as I confess openly that I can be a bully at times with my strong opinions. Just because I have one does not mean I have to bulldoze my way into thinking I am the solution, even if my opinion does hold some merit. It is always better to be invited into a conversation. This is hard work, and I do not always succeed, but as I have said, my loved ones remind me of my promises to use my ears to listen instead of my mouth to advice.

We all want and need to be heard, loved, respected, and validated. This is our nature. Maturity that comes from our disappointments helps us to define the light source, commit to it, and learn to respect it. My biggest disappointments provide my best learning, teaching me that something grander is waiting for me just around the bend as I journey through my life. Trusting you are loved from a source that does not always uncover all that awaits you, beloved child, is never easy. We as humans tend to always want to take all matters into our own hands creating what we think is best. The facts are, we cannot always see our own future; we are too emotionally involved; we tend to lose focus on our gift of insight. Spirit has that covered in conjunction with committed Spirits of lost loved ones having a personal stake in our happiness. It is an investment for Spirit Source, as well as your own designated source. Remember always, we are a team and as a team we all need to learn how to listen to ourselves and each other, in flesh as well as in Spirit.

Disappointments cause dark moments and can last longer than they need to. Remember, the power of dark energy exists and wants to regain and remain in control. Allowing disappointments to linger without resolve allows this energy to remain in control of your power. The dark energy wins, keeping you in shackles in this prison of darkness you are creating in your disappointments. Shed the light on this as quickly as possible. Take the time to grieve and address your disappointments that are stirring your emotions. Release them to the light, knowing this light will release you, unbinding your inflictions, allowing your whole sense of being to transition to a peaceful state resulting in, as well as sustaining, core stability.

Part Three

Journeys Out of Darkness

FINDING LIGHT IN THE DARKNESS

People say many incredible things when loving Spirit moves them. I feel very blessed to bear witness to this kind of reaction every day in my life. It allows me to be right in the middle of a promise that Father Spirit and I made together. I promised to do His work at every opportunity that is presented to me, and Spirit promised to show up and present messages of healing, insight, and miracles, gifting the person exactly what they requested. This is just the way my days play out. From the moment I open my eyes until the end of my day, I am aware of Spirit moving within me. I have learned to accept and embrace my life with this work I said "yes" to the calling, the events, and the outcomes. I want to share some of these special moments with you, my readers. Some of you may be new to the idea of sharing the whole truth. Some of you are just awakening to the Spirit world.

Coming to life in your consciousness and awakening in Spirit, may inspire you to heighten your internal happiness in the grandest way. This may feel foreign or strange as it reaches new heights, encouraging you to try new things or to be open to ideas or concepts you may not have given much thought to in the past. You can feel a movement within that is stirring your whole essence in a new direction. Perhaps you will share something personal with a stranger, bringing up and feeling strong emotions. Maybe you will step out of your comfort zone and speak out about something you may have kept to yourself. You may notice changes that seem uncomfortable, comparable to growth, but more of an internal stirring deep inside your heart. This is what I call a "Spiritual awakening."

Spiritual awakening can cause you to have a vast appetite for books, for knowledge more aligned with anything ranging from psychic ability including palm reading, crystals, tarot cards, celestial, astrology, Reiki, Shamanic practices, or meditation. We are all different and as we awaken, we all will be searching for our own personal prana, our soul food.

This is a time in your life to celebrate your commitment to the Spiritual part of your heritage that is connecting you to your Source. This Source is wise and knows you so completely that if you ask, you will be directed to what resonates in you. All the hunger you feel will be quenched if you only stop in silence long enough to ask for your gifts to be revealed. Of course, we are never left to fend for ourselves. We all have teachers, mentors, Gurus, guides. As you awaken in the stages of your growth, you will know exactly who your teachers will be. They literally just show up. Because of your growth, you will know without a doubt that they have been put in your life, directly on your path, for exactly what you need at the exact time you need it.

I have been very blessed with many healers, guides, and teachers on my journey. One of my first teachers was a layperson and right-hand to my parish priest. She taught me the gift and the power of Grace. Another teacher taught me how to survive in a world I knew nothing about. This stage of awakening was harsh for me at the time, and she taught me not to be so naïve to the world and that not everyone had good intentions. Another teacher stayed by my side for several years, teaching me and attuning my Reiki degrees. Another guru taught me the clarity and dedication that meditation provides me. I have had ordinary and extraordinary examples of teachers who have come directly from Spirit. The more I have grown in this lifestyle of acceptance of the power both flesh and Spirit provide for me, the more open I have become to new teachers who arrive in my daily interactions with others. I also have many Spiritual teachers, Archangels, and the power of the Trinity always by my side.

I would like to share with you a recent interaction involving connection, growth, awakening, awareness, Divine intervention, and healing power. Joe and are not really ones to book a holiday to an all-inclusive resort. We are the type who like to travel more in a rustic, rural experience. We are interested in modest lodging and local food in small local eateries. We love to explore the native environment and talk to real people living in modest simplicity. It was unusual for Joe and me to book a resort type of vacation, but we like to try new things and were easily persuaded to book a short four-day, five-night vacation in Cuba with our dear friends.

I had been to Cuba several years earlier and truly loved the beaches, which are some of the best in the world, the culture, the history, and the people. I enjoyed learning about their way of life in a Communist country. My impression of the Cuban people was that they were just like the rest of the world's population: broken and surviving. I was very excited for Joe to have the same experience I had had many years ago. As it turned out, he loved everything about Cuba.

As for me, I am always working and am never off the clock, even on vacation. I think it is because Spirit is never on vacation either. When you say "yes" to Spirit, you can never just shut it off, unless of course you are sleeping, and even then, you are awakened by thoughts, dreams, or messages.

While at the resort in Cuba, we met two women I instantly felt called to love. There was something very special about these women and the extended family they were spending time with. We introduced ourselves and talked about our work. Conversation flowed easily between us as we lounged around in the pool for hours. During our conversation, I was told that one of the women, Kelly, had a swollen hand. I asked if I could hold her hand for a moment. She agreed, and I was able to administer Reiki for a few moments during which an incredibly powerful connection with formed between us. I knew she was special and loved deeply by Spirit, although I felt she had forgotten that fact while facing the hardships of life. This is what Kelly had to say about our meeting in her own words.

Kelly's Message

I feel them always, sometime a hand on my head! I know this is my Dad! The smell of perfume or just that person whom you know their distant smell! My Dad was Old Spice; my Mum was soap only as she was allergic to perfumed items. Sometimes I see pictures in nature like this one I just shared with you. I hear dogs and cats crying, bobcats, and fishers. I feel like I walk one with nature. I feel the winds as I listen to Mum's words shared through whispers in the leaves. Then, poetry spews from my heart. I love because I do, I then embrace it. When you held my hand, I felt an opening in my heart. Your words, your strength, your love shows me a way to another side of me. There is a place I would like to show you: A meadow. I think you have seen it. I know this may sound weird, but I took you there in a dream. We could have a book release party at my restaurant. I would love it if you guys would come and visit me at our cottage. I feel you are the one to quiet the minds of those who are troubled or those who see the world as an enemy; those who only know the superficial moment of monetary gain; those taking advantage of all they can. I know your inspiration, and your healing will bring people who are in pain back to reality. I truly share this common heart with you.

From the first moment you looked into my eyes, I knew we would be connected forever! Thank you for hearing and sharing your wisdom with the world. You, I know, your wisdom will touch many people's lives and change them forever. We can all do this; we already recognize that when you have this experience you become the example of this same experience. You become internally what you have written about and for this cause, its authentic love.

Kelly's poem:

There are those who simply touch your hand
That gift touches your soul
The healing of love
That touches every part of you
It is a gift of love
A gift of passion
That could, if you listen, show you the way
The real you
The one under your skin
The one that is itching to get out
One that is asking to be released
If only someone would listen

Kelly has discovered she, too, has this same gift. When you recognize yourself in the eyes of another, you are seeing the reflection and the truth of your own loving essence shining back at you. Kelly, you are all this truth in all you write. Kelly deserves this same self-love and recognition she saw in my own soul. Yes, you are love, loved, and worthy. Thank you from the deepest part of me for sharing your words of passion and truth, for having the courage it took to write it, and for sharing your beautiful Spirit, your light emanating from you that shines in our world. You have helped us heal in more ways than you know by being a brave example of your sharing. This action of inspirational intention heals all wounds, birthing true peace to the living.

Sharing our journey as we did, this connection of light gave us the power to release darkness, creating healing within. Kate will share more of her journey below and her Cuban experience. Finding light in the darkness is never easy. These women understand the power of suffering and loss. These women, who are great friends, love each other, and both have had to pick up the pieces and carry on. When I met them, it was an instant tugging between our hearts and souls. They are warrior women dancing to their own unique rhythm that life has brought to them. I have been blessed with this new connection we share. We all love without conditions and we will cross paths again. We will pick up where we left off, celebrating in the joy of living life to the fullest. I have been blessed to have had these women offer to share their personal experiences, and I encourage each one of my readers to bravely reach out and connect with someone to whom you feel called to extend a kind thought, a hand, and your heart. You just never know what treasures lie within you waiting to be discovered through a stranger who may help you find light in the darkest part of you. This interaction may allow you to shine brightly, leading the way, spreading light in the darkness. That light, the start of your beautiful future, may be just around the corner. How exciting! I know you are destined for the full experience, and I know it takes courage to trust your heart. I also know I believe in you!

Kate, most certainly, has something magical about her. I could sense her energy before she even spoke to me. I could tell just by being in her space that she was special, that she rarely allowed herself to shut down, that she was wise beyond her years and a survivor. I watched her speaking with my friend, deep in conversation, and remember knowing this about her before being introduced to her. My friend, Susan is a maven. By own proclamation, true to the meaning, she is a connector from source to source. So, within a short time, we found ourselves congregating in the big pool chatting away getting acquainted. I asked Kate to share her experience of Cuba with you.

Kates Message:

One thing that I have always believed in is that when someone is hurting so badly, and they fail to seek the help they need, the healer will find them. This is what happened to me. My husband died over eleven years ago. It melted the core of me. I could not even allow myself one moment to move towards seeking out any kind of healing for myself. I could not even say his name without dropping like a ball and sobbing. But I had a business to run, a young child to raise, and all the stresses in life to deal with. There was no time to allow myself the healing I required. But as I said the healer will find you.

This is how she did it. I was in Cuba at a great resort with my best friend and family. As we sat around the pool talking and laughing, I encountered a woman who just had a beautiful smile and exuded an incredible Spirit about her. We started chatting about just everyday things. After a bit she said, "Oh here comes my best friend Tracey." She told me the minute she met Tracey she knew she had to be friends with her. And such sweet best friends they are! Full of care and love for one another, which was apparent from the time Tracey arrived on the scene.

Tracey is just surrounded in light. She would be handy on a dark forest trail to lead the way. Her light shines that bright! You just cannot ignore it. And once she shares a little bit of it you just want more. After a little small talk, she looked at me and said, "Who is that tall, handsome fellow you have with you?" I sort of looked behind me and there was no one. So, I asked who she was talking about. I had been told many times that he was always with me. I told her that I had lost my husband a number, of years ago and it was probably him. She confirmed it indeed was. At that moment I wanted to cry, in fact I think I did. She told me she had many things to say but felt that this was not the time due to several factors. I was fine with that as I did not want to break down at that moment.

While at the resort I had booked an appointment for a massage. Not something I would normally do. As I made my way to the off beaten path spa, I kept asking myself why I booked a massage here. As I knew in my head that my massage therapist had ruined me for anyone else. But massage I did. It was not one of the best massages I had ever had but just thought, "Oh well Kate, listen to your instincts next time." I decided to wait for my sister-in-law, who was going next for her massage down at the spa, therapy salt, and water pool.

As I came down the steps and around the bend to the pool, I saw Tracey and her best friend, and their husbands. I knew immediately that this is the true reason I had made the massage appointment. I was there to meet up with Tracey. Tracey called me over and asked me to sit with her. What then happened was one of the top ten most beautiful things that has ever happened to me. Tracey explained that I was holding on to a piece of my husband that was binding him to me, making it impossible for him to move freely to do good things for me and our son which was preventing me from really healing. She assured me that he loved me and would always be with me, but we had to release the piece that I was holding onto. As she led me through the process (which I will not tell because everyone has their own healing and no two are the same). It was so emotional and uplifting. Tracey made me feel safe, confident, and loved during this process. I knew immediately that she had helped with this release. I felt lighter, happier, and knew I could mention my husband's name without crying. To this day I have only cried once on the anniversary of his death. Funny, I even feel him around more than I ever did. I know personally he has saved from me two different occasions where I was in danger. He is with me. He is in my heart, but free to roam. And I have made a most amazing friend.

I am much more intentional in the way I love. I am closer to my own family who could never understand my pain. I am a happier person and able to move on to the possibility of finding another partner to finish my time on this earth with. But I always know that Rand is with me and supports me in all I do. He usually appears at my window in the form of a cardinal when he is not happy with a decision I made. He dives bombed the window a million times trying to tell me so.

Tracey, I say to you

Tracey L. Pagana

"Life isn't about waiting for the storm to pass…. It's about learning to dance in the rain"

Vivian Greene

Thank you for helping me dance in the rain again. I love you and I know I am blessed to have met you and have you in my cheering circle. I will forever remember the day the healer found me, Kate.

I have invited some more very brave people to write a bit of their own coming out of darkness moments and how they have helped them grow from this place of despair into a place of illuminated hope.

The next few chapters are dedicated to other strong ambassadors of truth who have found their light, their truth, coming out of their own struggles and darkness. They had the courage to share a small piece of their journey hoping to shed their healing light for others seeking wholeness. Some of these chapters will speak directly to your heart space and some directly to your soul. Reading these chapters, I have been touched by their courage and their desire to help others by sharing personally.

CHOOSING THE LIGHT: MY JOURNEY

Choice. A simple concept, but sometimes not an easy thing to do in certain circumstances.

Choice is unavoidable most days because it is a key component of life. For example, you choose what to order off the menu of your favorite lunch spot. You decide whether to go out with your friends for a drink or stay home and catch up on your Netflix watch list. These choices are relatively easy to make, but when it comes to the big stuff, the act of choosing reveals its true nature. It is not as easy as deciding what flavor of tea you want from Starbucks or what accessories to wear. The big stuff includes earth-shattering decisions. Stuff like, do you stay in the relationship you know makes you unhappy, because it is easier to stick together financially? Do you choose to remain at your job, even though you feel so drained after work you just want to curl up in bed and cry? Do you cut out that family member (or friend) that is toxic, knowing full well it will be one of the hardest things you will ever have to deal with? Suddenly, when faced with life-altering decision-making, the simple 6 letter word of choice seems a far more daunting task. And when I hit my rock bottom, I had to ask myself: do you choose to live in the light, or do you choose to be overtaken by the dark?

As I navigated through the beginning stages of my teen years, the darkness came knocking and I answered the door, if not a little too eagerly. It presented itself in the form of rebellion.

I was emotionally drained from my unstable childhood and from impossibly rigid expectations. Combine that with an absent father and a lack of love and empathy and it is a textbook case for why I chose to start living a high-risk lifestyle. My emotional health had started declining at a very young age and got progressively worse until I was diagnosed with depression at the age of 15.

As a young child I was in tune with those around me. I could pick up on the emotions of children, adults, and even animals. I was eight years old the first time I recall seeing Spirit manifest as a young boy, sitting across from me at the dinner table I was sitting at, doing my homework. My mother had left with my baby brother to do errands and I was left alone in the house. I, of course, did not know what to make of it. I certainly didn't realize that I was different in this ability, and I began to tell my friends 'ghost stories' of all the things I had experienced. I quickly became a bit of a weirdo among the children my age and learned to be selective to whom I shared this knowledge with.

As I aged, the visions of Spirit intensified. I had many experiences that I tried to reason with myself did not happen. There was always something inside me that made me question myself and try to apply logic to explain away the experiences. Despite the doubt, I think I always knew in my heart that I was seeing and feeling things for a reason. I felt I had a greater sense of purpose, a pressure to do something more in my life. Unfortunately, the light within me began to flicker and burn out as the darkness swooped in. I was struggling to stay afloat and finally I gave in to the shadows.

This period, which lasted approximately 3 years, is very hazy. This is the darkest period of my life to date. It was a time when I became greedy and overindulgent. It was a time of promiscuous sex, partying, and drug use. I abused drugs almost daily and my life revolved around getting my fix, whatever that may be. I was not picky. If not ecstasy or cocaine, then prescription drugs would do the trick. I would have violent, angry outbursts and cared little for anyone except myself. I was completely and utterly disconnected from myself and my true Spirit. I do not even know who I was. Thankfully, I do not have many memories from this time. But what I do know, I am not proud of. I was trying to push the inner child deep down inside. Her and her unresolved conflicts were not part of who I wanted to be as an adult. But like most things, there is a breaking point.

I recall begging the Universe to help me stop what I was doing. I truly believe that one must be careful what they ask for, because you just might get the help you need but not in the way you expect. The Universe granted my wish, and on August 4, 2006 as I walked home from a party where I had gotten extremely intoxicated, a complete stranger sexually assaulted me in an upper-class neighborhood where I thought I was safe.

The sad end to that tale is that the police did not believe me because of the drugs I had in my system. I was intoxicated and walking by myself late at night, after all. What did I expect? I was wearing a skirt.

Ask and ye shall receive. With this gift I was granted, I realized I was better than what the police had made me out to be. I quit the drugs cold turkey, which was hell, but I clawed myself out of the black hole. Although the light still was not its brightest, it was something. As I adjusted to sober living, I began to experience Spirit again. I could feel Spiritual presence in places I visited. I tried to use logic to tell myself these things were not really happening, but validation kept presenting itself. Every time I had a reading by a psychic, they would ask me why I was not using my gifts. I would have a dream about someone I had not seen in years. The urge would be so strong to contact them that in some cases I would, and they happened to be going through a difficult time and needed to hear from someone. I began trying to open myself to the experiences and messages and my light began to glow a little brighter.

I met Tracey in June of 2019 and she completely changed my life. I truly believe it was fate, but I will let you be the judge. It started with a reconnection between me and my friend Kate. We had ended our friendship three years earlier and it did not end on a good note. She was going through a difficult time and was exploring Spiritual healing.

I was working on myself through therapy. My therapist had suggested something unconventional to aid in my healing: inner child work. Within a week of this suggestion from my therapist, Kate called me on the phone and asked if I would consider seeing a Spiritual healer named Tracey. I was not really sold, but then she mentioned the buzzword that jolted me into knowing I had to meet Tracey: inner child work.

I made an appointment and instantly felt at ease the minute I arrived and locked eyes with her. Something magical happened in her healing room. In just one session, I felt 100 pounds lighter. It was exactly what I needed; it was so freeing. I was finally at peace with everything that I had been through. I left with the additional knowledge from Tracey and her beautiful guidance that I am a being that operates in the white light, and I have gifts that I can unlock to serve a greater purpose. It was the validation I had needed my entire life. Tracey also explained to me that I am an Earth Angel, and when I researched what this means I knew nothing was truer in my life than this. The description hits on every element of my life and personality. Knowledge is a beautiful thing! After my session I knew it was time to make a choice; it was time to decide to live in the light, but always remember and respect the darkness. For me, it is about balance. You cannot have light without dark, good without bad. Each serves its own unique purpose. The most important message I can leave you with is that choices are there waiting to be made every day. What will you choose?

RECLAIMING MY WORTH

I would like to start by thanking Tracey for this opportunity to share my story. I have heard the statement, "When the student is ready, the teacher will appear." This statement resonates with me, for I was the student and Tracey the teacher. And a wonderful, patient, and loving teacher she is, and I, a very determined and courageous student.

I began seeing Tracey in March of 2019. Our initial meeting would be the beginning of four months of intense healing. Every week, I addressed and released more and more childhood trauma.

Being born into darkness would describe my childhood experiences. My father was an alcoholic and physically and mentally abusive. My mother was just existing, her Spirit having been broken long before I came along. She, my mom, took the bulk of the physical and mental abuse and left my father several times with her children, only to end up going back again. And there were times when she left without us because of threats from my father.

The environment I was raised in was so negative and violent that my siblings and I would run and hide when dad came home. We would literally keep an eye out, and when one of us saw him we would inform the others. We never knew what to expect. Often, my youngest brother and I would watch our dad beating mom in case mom needed help. As it happened, my oldest brother, who is 15 years older than I, learned to be just like dad. I witnessed him beating up a man so badly that I stood there in shock, not being able to move.

One of my father's drinking buddies had molested me at a very young age. There was no one to tell but my siblings, for mom was not there at the time. Even if she had been, I still probably would not have told her. I got used to keeping things to myself and dealing with things internally. When you get blamed for everything, you start to believe you are the problem, even though you tell yourself that you are not. Somewhere deep inside, I felt worthless, not outwardly, but subconsciously.

Fast forward to what brought me to Tracey. I had just ended relationship on one and one-half years with a non-abusive alcoholic, who we will call George. A year before that, my son and I gotten into a huge argument and had not spoken since. I was feeling extremely unhappy, angry, disappointed, and depressed. I was given Tracey's number and that is where my healing started.

Through my sessions with Tracey, I have come to realize that I had a pattern of picking men who would disappoint me, and this would give me a reason to leave the relationship. This, of course, was done on a subconscious level.

My relationship with my son was the result of my own shortcomings. Because I had come to believe I was worthless, I had projected these feelings onto him. It was never done in malice or with the intent to harm. I was making decisions and choices from a place of brokenness, for lack of a better word. I would feel so guilty and ashamed of things I said and did to him. I knew it was wrong; I knew I did not like what I was saying and doing, but I did not know how to stop or change my behaviour. I now realize how guilt, shame (personal and family shame), and fear have kept me trapped in darkness. It is only by walking through the shame, the guilt, the regret, and the pain of it all that healing can take place.

I am telling my story not through a victim's eyes, but through the eyes of a warrior. I did not go through all of this without learning very valuable lessons. I do not blame my father anymore for my life being the way it is. I do, however, hold him accountable for his actions and behaviour when I was a child, as I am responsible for mine. I have found the peace that comes from forgiveness. Not only did I realize I needed to forgive my father; I also realized I had to forgive myself for believing and accepting all the lies that were told to me. Had I not believed I was worthless; I would not have been able to project that onto my son. For that too, I forgive myself.

It is important to understand that things happen for a reason. I do not believe in coincidences or random occurrences. I believe the Universe and God brings people and circumstances into our presence as an opportunity to heal. I have come to realize that if I am reacting to something in an emotional way, whether the emotion is good or bad, it's my emotion and I am the only one who is in control of how I am choosing to react. I have learned to take back my power by being accountable for my own actions and my own feelings. That is freedom! Freedom from identifying with the opinions and feelings of others.

I believe circumstances unfolded the way they did to bring me to this place of peace and acceptance. The ending of an unhealthy relationship with George and the disconnection with my son were blessings in disguise. I am very grateful to them both, for they were the catalysts for my change.

I am also grateful and happy to say my relationship with my son has been transformed. We are both consciously aware now, and we no longer feel the need to place blame. Instead, we take full responsibility for our own feelings and our own happiness. I am so grateful to have such a loving, kind, intelligent, and forgiving son.

None of this was easy, by any means. Having to be completely honest when looking at and owning your own shit is painful! But the result is so worth it! I can now look back on my childhood memories without the emotional attachment. I no longer identify with those old emotions that once use to define me.

When I left home, the abuse continued, not at the hands of my father, but by me. I continued the abuse by reliving the emotional pain attached to the memories. It is quite humbling to realize that I, too, played a big part in my own suffering. By sharing my story, it is my intent to help free others. Hopefully, it will give others the courage and strength to walk through their storms.

Thank you again, Tracey, for this opportunity. I would also like to give thanks for all the personal encounters throughout life, for without them, I would not be the person I am now! I would like to end my story with a beautiful comment from Ram Dass, a Spiritual leader who just recently passed on. Every person who comes into our lives "is just walking us home." There will be different interpretations of this message, but for me it means that all my encounters with people throughout life were meant to be, in order for me to acknowledge and reclaim my own worth, to be 'home' again, comfortable in my own identity and not trapped in the identity others want to place on me. So freeing!!!

COMING OUT OF DARKNESS IS SOUL WORK

Reflections by Linda Weir, founder of Expedition Inner Wisdom Inc.

"Into the forest I go to lose my mind and find my soul."

John Muir

I had barely explored one square foot of the festival's space when I received the call. I almost did not bother answering my phone. It had taken us 17 hours of driving the day before to get to Fayetteville, Arkansas, and I had a very limited amount of time to check out this Goddess Festival that I had read about weeks earlier in my office up in Canada. This trip was all about my son and his upcoming enrollment at the University of Arkansas. I was merely trying to squeak in an hour of my scarce, unscheduled time to explore what a goddess festival might look like since I had never been to one, and to experience how folks in a southern state in the USA might deliver one. Things of a Spiritual nature had, since I could remember, always piqued my interest.

"Hello," I said into my cell phone as I continued to walk about the festival grounds, examining displays and items placed strategically on tables.

"Mom." It sounded almost more like a question than a salutation. I could tell by his voice it was my oldest son – a responsible and sensitive young man in his mid-twenties at that time.

"Hi Alex!"

"Mom." Again, I noted this odd kind of hesitancy to his voice.

"Yes, Alex."

"Mom." Okay, now I knew. He was afraid to tell me why he had called. This sort of thing had not happened before, but I knew what he was about to say was causing him a huge amount of distress, so I quickly flipped into my mother-who-creates-a-safe-space mode.

"Alex, it does not matter what it is you have to say. I am your mother. I love you, will always love you, and could never stop loving you, no matter what words you ever

82

said and no matter what actions you ever took. I am, and always will be, forever yours."

"Mom."

"Yes, Alex. Just go ahead and say it. It is okay. I can handle it."

"Your mom died. Your sister found her deceased in her home."

Still in that mode of wanting to make things easier for my son, I replied, "Oh, she is probably just sleeping." It sounds silly, I know, but my instincts to make it easier for my son overrode common sense.

Alex's bravery had been unleashed. He now took on the role of the caring adult. "No, Mom. There is no mistake." His voice was compassionate and full of gentle strength. "Your mom has passed away."

My mother's death was sudden and very unexpected.

Still being in the frame of mind to hold the space for others, I finished my call with Alex by reassuring him that I was okay, that his grandmother had loved him very much, and that I would be on my way home promptly. Then, for fear that the festival organizers might misinterpret why I was so abruptly leaving their festival after having spent less than a few moments there, I briefly explained the situation to them. They offered their condolences, and I slipped outdoors into the parking lot.

It took mere seconds for me to find and lean against one of the few trees dotting the paved landscape. The moment my back rested against the bark of the tree – that moment where I became physically supported by this beautiful expression of nature – I let go of every inkling to stay stoic or strong. I knew I was in the arms of the purest form of unconditional love and support. The tree - an uncensored, unedited extension of the Divine - had my back, not just physically, but also in an unmistakable Spiritual way. In the tree's embrace, I knew to my core that I could withstand this bombshell and survive. The strength of something much bigger than myself fortified me. I stepped forward into the hours and days ahead of mourning and grief.

It would be months later, while spending some meditative time reflecting on my life, that I could see more clearly how profoundly trees and nature had played such a pivotal role in my Spiritual journey. When I was a small child, likely no older than 6 years of age, I recall riding my bike down to a small, wooded area at the end of our street. There, by a tiny brook, I would spend hours speaking with a Divine power that I intuitively knew had created every element of the natural world – plants, animals, rocks, clouds, and me! I felt as though my home was not on this planet, but up in the sky with this Divine power and that the trees, birds, streams, mountains and more were all pure expressions of this sacred, omniscient, eternal force, and because nature offered a pure, unaltered expression of this celestial entity, I got the sense that by connecting with the natural world, I received a direct line of communication with this loving presence. Comfort and companionship also filled me when spending time with the trees, plants, and animals because they felt like brothers and sisters to me.

Over the years, intimate moments with nature have sustained me and given me the close connection to Source, to God, that I crave as I navigate my way through this human experience. A visit to my home reveals a myriad of representations of trees. I have paintings of trees, sculptures of trees, and plates, napkins, cups, coasters, and more with trees on them. My property rests on a half-acre treed lot covered with beautiful old oaks and pines, to which I have added an additional thirty or more trees in the last year, and when I am not busy tending the yard, I am off across the street on the trails of a provincial park. For me, if I want to get close to God, I get close to nature.

SPEAK YOUR TRUTH

USE YOUR VOICE

Written with love and light by Kelli Fraser

For God…. Who makes all things possible!
Mark 10:27

My heartfelt acknowledgement and sincere gratitude to Tracey for her support of my healing, for her encouragement to remember the truth of who I am, and for creating the space for me to share my story. The words below are my written testimony of my own life and my journey of moving from darkness to light!

"Fear not, for I am with you; be not dismayed, for I am your God. I will strengthen you, yes, I will help you."
Isaiah 41:10

It can take an entire lifetime to find your way back to the truth and the essence of who you really are. It is my belief that we all begin with love and light, and we radiate this light to all we encounter. We are a presence, a true miracle, a physical representation of God's Divine love. We are God's precious gifts to this world. Each one of us is a child of God yet created with our own unique handprint. We are created by love, filled with God's love, and we begin with love.

If you have ever had the opportunity to watch a child discovering his or her own world around them, you understand that to see the world through a child's eyes is truly magnificent. Children approach this world with pure innocence, believing and trusting that it is a safe place and that the people surrounding them not only love them, but would never do harm to them. Carrying this belief along with them, they embark on their path of learning.

My God teachings: I give thanks to my Irish Grandmother, Annie Keough, for planting the seeds that God loves me, is always with me, and will always be there for me. All I must do is reach for him and ask.

My Grandmother's steadfast and unwavering faith, despite her life of hardships, laid the very foundation for my own relationship with God. For loving me the way that she did, and for blessing me with such a gift, I am eternally thankful. Even though she

85

died when I was just a young girl, the influence she had on my life was a powerful one. She was a brave woman who persevered and met life head on with sheer determination. She fully embodied the meaning of what it is to be a survivor. Even though she had left me, in the physical realm, I have always felt her strong presence in my life.

I began to reach for God at a very young and tender age. It was at a time when I felt completely alone, when I was full of fear and searching for a safe place. I had remembered the whispers of my grandmother's voice and trusting all that she had instilled in me, I asked God to watch over me and protect me. In God, I found a place of refuge, a sanctuary, a lighthouse lighting my way in a horrific storm.

My mother was my grandmother's second youngest of ten children. This was not uncommon in a remote town in Eastern Canada largely inhabited by Irish descendants. When my mother became pregnant at the age of 17 and unmarried, it was my grandmother who opened her home to us, providing a foundation for my mother and me to start our lives together. It was while my grandmother was in ill health and dying that my mother met my abuser. Little did any of us know that this man would impact all our lives in such a devastating way; the same man who promised my grandmother on her death bed that he would take good care of her daughter and granddaughter.

My stepfather began abusing me sexually when I was three years old. My first recollection was of him fondling me in the bathtub. He would insist on my always sitting in his lap, wanting me to kiss him. He would tell me that I was his special girl, tell me how beautiful I was and how much he loved me. I trusted him. I gave him the precious gift of my innocence. He would sneak into my bedroom at night, while my mother was sleeping, and he would get under the covers with me. I would often be awoken, in the middle of the night to my stepfather touching me. He would tell me that it was our special time together and that no one needed to know about it. He would tell me this had to be kept a secret from my mother because she would be very upset, and if she were to ever find out, she would kill herself. The love that I felt for my mother was immense. I adored her. My mother was my entire world. Her unconditional love was what had sustained me through this tumultuous time. I could never, ever, begin to imagine my world without her in it, so I kept our special secret for a very long time.

I was ten years old when I finally disclosed my abuse to a close family member. I innocently asked her, "Does your dad ever touch you?" The look that came across her face is one that I will never forget. I pleaded with my older cousin, "Please don't tell my mom!" I had lived in fear of my mother ever finding out this painful secret, a secret that I had shared with my stepfather and had kept locked away inside of me for so long. The very thought of my mother ending her life was something that I could not even bear to think of. I cherished my mother. She was all I had. My world revolved around hers. How would I ever survive this life without her?

My stepfather would purposefully orchestrate situations where he could be alone with me, and any time that he was successful in doing so, he would sexually abuse me. After he violated me in this way, he would continue his routine as though nothing had happened. As a child, I could not comprehend what was happening to me. I could not resolve inside myself why I was forced to keep this from my mother, and I started to carry the burden of guilt for not telling her. My feelings toward my stepfather began to feel very conflicted. I loved him because he was my dad, or at least the dad who chose to be in my life; however, I did not like what he was doing to me and, more importantly, how it was beginning to make me feel about myself. I started to feel a lot less like my dad's special girl as the years passed, and this feeling was replaced by many other negative feelings, mostly towards myself, but also directed at my stepfather. I could not begin to understand why, if he did, in fact, love me the way he always said he did, how he could possibly hurt me so deeply and irreversibly.

"In all things, trust God." More echoes of my grandmother's wisdom. I could hear her sweet voice in my head. So, I did. I prayed to God every night to please not let my stepfather come into my bedroom. He did, anyway. As the years went by, the negative feelings that I felt initially about myself and towards my stepfather grew far more intense. I felt such horrific shame for the things that he would do to me. Victims of crime take on responsibility for the crime committed against them. This was true not only of my own experience, but also of what I had witnessed in so many others throughout my life. I felt that I was bad, that I was dirty from the inside out. I felt like I must have done something horribly wrong to deserve this. I felt that there must be something terribly wrong with me. I felt disgust not only for my stepfather, but also towards myself. I felt worthless and devalued. My relationship with God began to fade away. I felt that God did not care about what I was going through. I felt abandoned and betrayed by everyone around me. I felt that God had forgotten all about me, and I felt completely alone.

When a child has experienced sexual violence, its damages are catastrophic not only to the physical body, but also to the mind and soul. As a young person, it is impossible to fathom the magnitude of this impact to your whole psyche. This often results in distorted thoughts and messages about yourself. These distorted thoughts turn into distorted core beliefs and, eventually, become your reality. I believed many untruths about myself, including the core belief that I was damaged and, therefore, unworthy of love. Those negative feelings that had erupted inside of me so long ago continued to follow me for most of my life, robbing me not only of the peace, love, and joy that I deserved, but also of the many blessings God had intended for my life, stealing pieces of myself that I will never recover. My stepfather took my childhood from me, leaving behind a very broken person. Some of these distorted core beliefs remain with me to this very day, and on the days, I struggle, they can sneak in like a stranger in the night to torment me.

Guilt, fear, and shame are commonly experienced by many child sexual abuse survivors. Most survivors blame themselves for their own abuse. As an adult child of sexual abuse, you constantly fight to not believe the lies you were told about yourself or came to believe about yourself. Shame holds us hostage. It holds you back from reaching your potential. You feel like a prisoner in your own life. Shame forces us to play "small," to retreat and hide.

Shame and fear have utterly consumed me throughout my life. I felt as though I did not know who I was without them. These negative emotions were so comfortable to me, like an old pair of shoes that molds to the shape of your feet. There have been times in my life that I admit, I have been crippled by my own fear. It swallowed me up. Fear has many faces and keeps us stuck in our pain. Fearful thoughts and feelings can overcome you, obscuring your truths. They cause you to forget not only the beauty that exists in the world, but also the beauty and the truth inside of you.

I have learned that there are different responses to shame and fear. Some people run from these painful feelings by staying insanely busy, preoccupying their thoughts, overachieving, and setting their bar to a level that is impossible to reach or attain. Others take a different approach and numb themselves by indulging in less-than-healthy coping mechanisms, such as food, gambling, alcohol, sex, and drugs. The unfortunate reality, however, is that no amount of running or numbing can erase the darkness that exists inside of you or eliminate those all-too-familiar feelings of unworthiness.

I honestly cannot remember when it was that I started running. Running away from my past, running from my shameful secret, my inner demons, and myself. I ran from all the pain including the overwhelming sadness, and the darkness that permeated my whole being. I ran in every direction that I could possibly think of, and, unfortunately, in ways that took me further and further away from my true self.

When my mother learned of my disclosure, she ended her relationship with my stepfather. She moved myself and my brother out of the province with her. It was when I started to feel safe in our new surroundings that I was flooded with horrific memories, terrifying nightmares, and extremely disturbing flashbacks. There were many nights that my mother held me in her arms and rocked me back to sleep to console me and make me feel safe. She would promise me, whether she believed it or not, that everything would be alright. I wanted so much to believe her. I tried so hard to act like a "normal" kid in a world where I never felt like I quite fit or really belonged.

The harder I fought to forget everything that had happened to me at the hands of my stepfather, the more I was chased and haunted by it. These awful ghosts would show up unannounced, devouring me, leaving me wounded and shattered.

My mother is the strongest and most courageous woman I have ever known. She is extraordinary. She lives life to the fullest and she loves people. She radiates love and kindness and gives of her heart in the most unselfish ways. People are drawn to her charismatic charm. She is a beautiful soul. It deeply saddens me that I have been witness to my mother's heartbreak at two significant times in my life. The first was when she learned of my disclosure, and the second was when the police notified us of my brother Rob's sudden and tragic death.

I never spoke a word during the sexual assaults against me. Over time, I had mastered the coping skill of retreating inward. I remember thinking that if I did not hear my voice out loud, that maybe what was happening to me was not real somehow. The deeper I would go inside of myself, the more I would imagine the most spectacular places where I felt safe and free. There was once this most extraordinary place where I was surrounded by a field of sunflowers. They were all at least six feet tall, with great big happy faces angled towards the sun. I ran through that field of sunflowers as fast as my legs would carry me, away from my stepfather, away from all of the ways he had hurt me, my bare feet touching the earth's surface below, the sun kissing my face, and the warmth of the wind at my back. I felt incredibly happy here, and I would return to this magical place many times to find an escape from my tortured reality.

It was during my years of violence against women work, where I had the opportunity to not only observe, but also witness the many symptoms and far reaching effects of child sexual abuse and molestation. Self-hatred is but one of the many negative effects of abuse, paving the way to self-destruction. I was certainly no exception to this rule. Self-loathing can take a person down some very dark alleyways. Darkness continues to spread throughout your being like a raging forest fire, burning everyone and everything it touches. My path of self-destruction carried on in my life for much longer than I would like to admit, and the personal costs have been many. I perpetuated my cycle of violence by continuing in abusive relationships where I was further victimized. This feeling was very familiar and comfortable to me, considering the fact these actions resembled my normal. I was, like other innocent victims, a product of what I had lived in my family of origin. I held on to the untruths about myself, the same negative core beliefs about myself from long ago, the false belief that I deserved what was happening to me, and that abuse was simply more of the same. I never expected anything else. I had learned the hard way that expectations only lead to being horribly disappointed. I stopped allowing myself to dream about anything good happening in my life, and when met with future abuse, it did not take me by surprise. It was predictable.

I looked for love and validation of my worthiness in all the wrong places, desperate to mend the broken places inside of me and to somehow make me feel whole, only to have my heart crushed over and over and my self-worth annihilated. Sadly, I remained in this destructive cycle for many years. Each failed relationship with others reinforced the painful untruth that I was to blame. That it was all my fault. That there had to be something wrong with me. These unhealthy relationships had served to support the false evidence of my distorted core beliefs about myself, and the more I hated myself, the more enmeshed I became in this messed-up cycle. I ran so fast from my painful past and what lingered of it, only to run right into more of it. I was living a pattern. I did not know anything different. Abuse was all I had ever known in my life, and when you do not know any better, you cannot possibly do any better.

There were many aspects of my life that had the appearance of "having it all together," from an outside perspective, that is. There were even times when I, myself, truly believed I had it all together. I graduated from high school with honours and was awarded a scholarship towards my post-secondary education. I was well educated, and I established a thriving career that I was passionate about. I had had a strong desire burning within me to help others, to bring about a difference in this world, the world that I had come to know as sad and disappointing, full of pain and loss, cruel and unjust. A world where love hurts, where you learn to not trust anyone, and you feel all alone.

"Be the change you wish to see in the world." These were wise words written by Mahatma Gandhi and are words I have come to live by. I worked in the Social Work field for many years, focusing on the area of Violence against Women and Children for over two decades. Based on my childhood, this work was not a stretch. I devoted my entirety, submerging completely to this battle taking place against women and children. It was my true heart's desire to protect the most vulnerable beings in our society. However, it is now my understanding that it was God all along, calling me to do this work. He knew I would dedicate my entirety to this work, and by living through my experiences, not only had I the necessary insight, but also the ability to reach so many others. I tried to be whatever I could possibly be for the people who needed my expertise. I took my work very seriously and gave a piece of myself to every single woman and child I advocated for. I believe I had a place in their healing journey, and they, too, had a place in mine, for we had, indeed, healed one another. When I look back on this work, even with its many challenges, I am so thankful to all the brave women and children who touched my life in such a meaningful way; who taught me so much about life, about grace, and about myself. May God bless you all!

God, so graciously, has blessed my life with two beautiful children to love. The love that I feel for them is impossible to put into words. They both are amazing human beings who have taught me so much about myself, and, most importantly, taught me how to love unconditionally. I felt God's love and light illuminate through me for the first time in a very long time with the blessing of these two very precious gifts of life. The love I received from my children filled me up in ways that reached down, touching me deeply inside, healing the many shattered pieces that remained in the damaged parts of myself. And yet, somehow, despite their sweet love, I still did not feel whole. There was still something missing. This void felt like a gaping hole inside of me.

Sadly, I stayed stuck in my own personal pain, stuck in this harmful pattern of abuse and dysfunction, and no matter how hard I would try, I could not seem to find my way out. I could not see any light amidst the darkness that enveloped me. The most devastating part of all was that, now, my precious gifts from God, who had brought so much joy into my life, were also stuck on this ride with me - the deep sorrow that I have carried in my heart, for this pain was enormous. My innocent children both were casualties in this existing war against myself. I was a train wreck headed for disaster.

It was at another painful and pivotal intersection in my life that I, once again, found the courage to reach for God. Through much personal prayer, meditation, and Spiritual growth, I began to realize that God had not forgotten me in the ways that I had convinced myself He had. In fact, He had never left me at all. It was my own distorted thinking that had fuelled this destructive belief. The truth is that I had felt let down by God, and I was the one who had put the distance between us. God helped me to discover, in the ways that only God can, that the only way back to myself was through accepting and trusting God's love for me. God's pure unconditional love paved the way for this process. He helped me to see that I had to stop running away from myself, because no matter where I ran, I stayed stuck in the places I was running from. I had to find my way back, remember the truth, of who I started out as: a child of God, filled with his pure light and love. I had to heal that broken little girl who was still grieving inside of me, and only I could do this, not only by acknowledging all that she had been through and how deeply she suffered, but also by giving her the love that she so desperately needed and sought out from others. I invited God into my heart and genuinely asked for his guidance and forgiveness in my life. I needed his help to forgive myself and to become willing to forgive others, understanding that through my forgiveness, I set myself free. It was God's love and light that had been missing in my life. This was the void in my life, the gaping hole that I felt. I had been living my life on autopilot, going through the motions of life, existing but not truly living. I was relying only on myself, enforcing my own will instead of praying for God's will in my life. God's love has healed and continues to heal the empty and broken places inside of me. He has shown me that I am, and always was, deserving of love. It was only when I truly believed that I was deserving that I received.

Today, my life is full of beauty. On my walk with God, I continue to grow in grace, knowing that I still have much to learn on this voyage and more growing to do. God has brought so much to my life: peace in my heart; a deep sense of joy; freedom from my burdens and the demons of my past; a kind, loving, accepting, and supportive husband. Healthier relationships surround me and now, He has blessed me with another precious child to love. The darkness that once consumed me, that I never thought I could escape, has been lifted in the only way that was ever possible: through God's loving light.

"Create in me a clean heart, O God, and renew a right Spirit within me."
Psalm 51:10

This opportunity has allowed me to "speak my truth, by using my voice." I feel so strongly about this statement that it is tattooed on my left forearm as a constant reminder that I am worth "healing love."

Part Four

Lessons from Spiritual Darkness

DARK VS LIGHT BOUNDARIES

My clients who feel they need to heal work hard in their sessions. We commit to and confide in each other on deeply personal matters. During our sessions we discover wounds and scars that have been buried so deeply they are hidden away, mainly so they are not felt. In my growing awareness, I have noticed that dark energy seeps into these pains and hurts. This makes it very difficult for people to release the emotions which often includes pain, sadness, fear, and anger. All these emotions feed dark energy, resulting in the dark energy expanding and overwhelming the individual. My work suggests ways of releasing these memories, experiences, and toxins. I know there are definite, designated boundaries for both light and dark energies, and both energies have significant power. As I have written in my first two books, I have personally struggled with both light and dark energy. These energies have been my biggest allies, as well as my biggest teachers. Both dark and light energies teach me their reasons for being present in my life.

Working with and shedding dark energy myself, as well as channelling for others, has taught me what dark energy represents. It is literally fed from negativity, greed, pain, anger, fear, instant gratification, tri-dimensional overstimulation, and obsessive behavior. This often results in an accumulation of unhealthy habits and addictions. Through the constant, repetitive experience of negative emotions, you unknowingly give permission to dark energy to become an intense, manipulative, controlling power over your life.

Through manic, unreasonable behavior, aggressive outbursts, low self-worth, depression, suppression, lies, and deception, energy has a very subtle, sneaky way of using your physical body to see what it needs and to hear what it wants. This power knows your human weaknesses. Trust me, this dark energy identifies your needs and desires in a very perceptive way. This energy might even suggest, "Oh, go ahead! Honestly, your actions are not really hurting anyone."

Most times dark energy speaks to you in a very seductive, subliminal, manner, creating so much noise in your world and in your head space, drowning out the truth and keeping you frozen in a comatose state. This energy is wise and sly and knows what it needs to keep you in the grasp of its power. This dark energy claims more power as it grows in a steady rate of destruction. It is real, and it is here to stay. This world is its domain, and it can lead many a heart and soul into its pit of despair. Simply talking about it gives me a cold chill as I pick my words to describe it very carefully.

I have engaged in this energy in the past by choosing selfishly. Reactions to my choices left me alone in a very dark place. I was caught in a seductive, slow dance and in a trap of deception of lies and good times. I was given things that sustained the needs of human flesh in experiences that felt good at the time. In many ways, I am very grateful for these experiences. The wisdom I gained provided me hands-on knowledge to be able to choose what energy I want to commit to and work with.

Dark energy has an agenda to gain more power and betray you. As it steals and gathers your power, it gains more power for itself. Its' purpose is to cause mass destruction through confusion and inflicting pain. It knows no boundaries and spares no person. It is a wake of destruction, greed, power, and carnage. It has no understanding of love; it only understands power. It will stop at nothing to gain what it needs, discarding weakness that does not serve it by stealing your power.

White light, on the other hand, is consciously and continuously aware of boundaries. Its boundaries surround you, shield you, protect you, and love you. White energy is always available. This energy is so aware of your independent lessons that it waits by your side silently, quietly waiting unless you ask for assistance. This energy is so in love with your essence, it waits to be invited before it steps in, joining forces to help you fight the darkness. This energy never leaves you. Even when you think you are desperately alone, this white light source, your soul essence, is never far away. There is nothing you could ever do that you would not be forgiven for if you were to ask with a true, sincere, honest heart.

Light energy is harder to attain than dark energy. It takes time and energy to commit yourself to cultivating, learning, and experiencing a certain way of life. This energy is our birthright. We are born from this energy and are made flesh to experience all forms of energies life offers. Light energy is everything good, kind and forgiving. We are a part of this energy that knows only one way of existence: unconditional love. This energy is always about giving thought, then action, resulting in love. Light energy has no fear and no limits. It has an endless abundance of acceptance and forgives in all ways, always.

White light energy embraces your whole being, saturates you with an army of love and protection so vast your breath would stop if you only knew the power of it. Receiving this love protects you, providing for you what you cannot see with a naked eye, but a glimpse of what you can feel with an open heart. I have come to personally know many of the Anointed Archangels and Spirits that come to work in session. These Spirits stand by their human charges, releasing their love and sending gifts to help soothe the broken people of this world.

I want to stress that this is my experience based on facts. This information is not fictional. I truly have had this experience between these two distinct powers. I have walked in darkness and taken a drink a few times from the cup of dark energy. The purpose for me was to have the experience so that I could advise and teach the difference between the two energies. I am grateful for this walk on the dark side; the lessons, the value, and the truth the dark energies taught me.

I need to make it very clear at this point that I do not ever work with or invite dark energy into my life. I have no use for it. I only work for my Divine, Spiritual Father. I have dedicated my life and my soul to the white light source. This loving energy supports me every day to help lead others out of dark spaces, releasing toxins that cause hidden scar tissue. It will be my lifelong mission to shed as much light as possible on this dark matter in hopes of bringing more light into what, at times, can be a very dark, troubled world.

SOUL FRIENDS

The previous chapter deals with a very touchy subject that can be difficult to process, so I thought I would lighten up and share with you some of my experiences with earth angels and people I call soul friends, starting with the difference these people have made in my life and how you might attain your tribe or group of like-minded, soul-connected people.

All I know is since I signed up to work my Spirit Father, it's like having a dad who lives right in the middle of my heart 24/7, consistently supporting me in a loving, incredible way. Not that my human "poppy" is not a beautiful source of wisdom and love; I just have the good fortune to have two.

My Spiritual Father teaches me in a different way, allowing me to think for myself and deal with the consequences of my choices. He has taken over where my poppy left off. My Spiritual Father did not start speaking up until first I acknowledged His existence and then started to ask specifically for His help. He has taught me to be responsible in a deeper way to my commitment and to be far more aware of the wisdom I ask for daily.

It has always been easy for me to make acquaintances. It seems the ability to attract people has always been something that comes naturally to me. People who know me might say I am not a shy person, but to be honest, I truly am, even though I am also a loud person. In truth, the louder I am, the less likely it is that I need to expose my vulnerability. In effect, my outgoing personality has been a shield of protection for my soft heart. If I could create the noise and dominate the conversation, I would have to share less about myself, my lack of education, and my poor choices. Smart, right? Sure, until you get caught or something embarrassing slips out, revealing a secret you were trying to protect.

I feel there are three distinct kinds of friendships: (1) Acquaintances; (2) Family; and (3) Soul Friends.

An acquaintance is someone you meet and feel a fondness for; a person who is interesting and someone you can learn from. Usually, an acquaintance comes into your life to teach you things. I do not usually invest emotionally in acquaintances, and they do not usually invest emotionally in me, which makes the coming in and going out of our lives an easier transition. There are no expectations or long-term commitments. When I think back over my life, I can see that I have learned important lessons from people who came into my life for a short time, for a specific purpose.

Family relationships can be difficult to navigate. The blood connection that you have with your parents, siblings, children, aunts, uncles, and cousins creates a bond, and ideally, you also become friends. However, at times, these relationships can feel like obligations rather than true, honest connections, and you may have to dig deep to find much in common. For me personally, my family relationships have shifted over the years, and I used to have considerably more contact with family than I do now.

The bond I have with my family is deep, but we are not as connected as we once were. When we were young, we did a lot of things as a family.   As we grew up and headed out on our own journeys, we grew apart in many ways. Nonetheless, the love I have for each one of my family members is strong, and the friendships we have are committed. If any one of us ever needed the other, all that would be required was a simple phone call or text, and we would respond.

Sometimes, family ties can be very difficult to sort out. My family was quite large and included very diverse personalities. I found it difficult to bond with my siblings, and even my parents, because I thought so differently than they did. I trying to find my way and make sense of life in general. Making decisions that affected not only me, but also my family, and learning some tough lessons along the way left me in some rather difficult situations. Feeling obligated to like your family can be a very tall order, when as a child, you were struggling even to like yourself. Liking our siblings is a choice many of us were not given as children and youth. We were told what to do and how to do it and what to feel, and those were the only options. If you obeyed and behaved, you were rewarded and if you did not, you were disciplined. As an adult, you come to understand the reasoning; as a child, I harboured the hurt, which made it very difficult for me to like my siblings as we fought our way through being heard and accepted in our home. What I learned from all of this, however, was how to forgive deeply, to appreciate the efforts of others, to work through tough life lessons, and to love each and every one of my family members for who they are.

Family dynamics may very well turn out to be your greatest teacher with respect to relationships. I have heard the saying many times that you cannot pick your family. You do have a choice to accept with love and forgiveness family members who provided you with both gifts and lessons. It is not my intent here to hurt any of my family. It is my intent only to describe the types of friendships I have developed in my life. I want to demonstrate that we can choose to shed light into our own dark places, to rise about situations and circumstances and experiences we do not like, and to love and support those in our circles. We are called to love, to forgive, and to find peace in the experiences that brought us painful lessons. Family, for some people, may provide a plethora of just these kinds of experiences.

Soul friends, on the other hand, are the best gift you could choose for yourself. Soul friends are gifts of living beings sent to you by Spirit. I believe my circle of soul friends and I have travelled together in many lives. I have been blessed over this lifetime to completely understand and accept the familiar concept that most of you most likely have heard: People come into your life for a reason, a season, or a lifetime.

Soul friends come into your life at the perfect time. There is an exact time and an exact moment they show up. I honestly do not know where I would be some days if I did not have these relationships, some going back over 50 years, others more recent. What defines these relationships is pure unconditional love and acceptance, no agenda, and a very strong commitment to respect each other and our boundaries. These relationships do not have room for ego, although there are times when we sort out ego and chat about topics that may bring out stimulating information. These relationships are mutually hand-picked and have only one intention: to stay connected in Spiritual growth.

I encourage you to take a moment to make a mental list of all the soul friends in your tribe. These people love you, respect you, console you, and counsel you, as you do them. I encourage you to find the strength and desire to seek out your tribe and find these soul friends who will teach you how to love and accept yourself and find true compassion. These relationships nourish you, feed you, and teach you how to trust and how to grow bigger than you ever knew you could.

IDENTIFYING YOUR SPIRITUAL GIFTS

I want to talk a bit about faith. Faith is something that is deeply personal. I have come to know faith as not just a work in progress, but the foundation of who I have become.

This energy I call faith has been growing within me, teaching me about the gift and its full meaning. I needed to commit to and invite faith into the core of my being. Faith has many meanings for me and teaches me awareness, providing me a safe place to digest and process all experiences of life. The faith journey is about finding faith within and then extending faith-filled love without holding anything back. Aligning faith, education, and action has been my primary secret ingredient, joined, of course, with loving Spirit Source. These ingredients, combined into thought and action, have taught me what faith feels like and what it represents. Faith born in me, alive within me, allows acceptance and gives me permission to embrace a true sense of whole self. Faith strengthens me, giving me permission to put myself first. Faith provides the opportunity to experience free-flowing, Spiritual, consistency-building momentum, as it cascades effortlessly, flowing freely from Divine Source within me.

Without faith as a primary ingredient as you are trying to discover your own awareness, you may struggle. Without faith, you are like an equation missing one of its components. How can you work out a mathematical equation if you do not have all the required information? Faith is the missing element of true self-knowledge and a requirement for Spiritual knowledge, aligning your destiny and the gifts you seek.

Faith will allow you the courage and quiet space required to address all pain, all growth, all acceptance all weaknesses, all truth. Faith provides you with grace and courage, as well as the wisdom you seek. You then have all your information. With an open heart, trust to ask Divine Source what your unique gifts are and how to own them, honing and molding them, gaining the loving wisdom your gifts provide you as they nourish you and teach you a new depth of whole self. This allows you to love and trust at the deepest level as you feel and live anew in connection with your loving Spiritual Father.

This energy has been waiting for you and will wait for you for all time. This energy loves its child, with every breath you take. This energy has patience and will wait as long as it takes for your faith to grow internally, so, you can receive your inheritance. Who has the right to imply you are not worthy, instilling fear, suggesting we may need to die in body before we may receive the rewards of Spiritual gifts? The Spirit-filled loving energy I work with and for every day does not teach me this. In fact, this energy encourages my growth, my love, and takes the veil of darkness off my eyes, allowing me to see as well as feel the living reality of its essence growing internally within myself. Even in my darkest moments, this light, this love, my faith, grow deeply in my own heart.

How to identify your own gifts is something that needs to resonate within the centre of your own truth, self-awareness, and convictions. It so personal that only you have the way, the means, and the tools to discover your gifts, uniquely and quietly calling you out of your own darkness as you seek your own truth and deep self-love. Let your faith in who you are define your awareness as it grows into a place of full-on acceptance. You are a beautiful, broken child, and your own unique essence combined with your brokenness, will lead you to your gifts. All you need to do is to allow them space within, accept them for the gifts they are, and forgive everything you need to release and everything you cannot control.

Rise above the pain, confusion, hurt, repercussions, and physical and emotional disabilities that are keeping you in a state of limbo. Accept your life, fully, passionately, and in the whole of the experiences you are living with and through. This takes a commitment of complete self-love, forgiveness, acceptance, integration, and collaboration in complete contract with your Divine Spirit. Know this as a bonus: your Spiritual Father has agreed to take all your burdens on, fully committing to the union you have.

I want to end this chapter in a positive light and share with you some snippets of a conversation with one of my soul friends. I do have her permission to do so. This friend has lived through a couple of years she would rather not repeat, as the pain of growing in those years completely exhausted her, drained her resources, and depleted her energy.

She and I have talked several times over the past couple of years about the kinds of things we need to invest in, teaching us how to identify not only our pain, but also the education required to work through the pain and the process of growth. We have collaborated often. We listen and support and advise each other, point out and validate, confirm, and digest the information we activate in each other as we try to overcome our hurdles. This friend is always close, not so much in space but in Spirit, as she stands and commits to her path, my path, and our defined boundaries and trust.

My Spiritual friend, in a conversation one day, asked me how she could know what her gifts were. I said, "Simply. Just ask." As she contemplated that answer, I could feel her digesting deeply what I had just said. You could tell in her silence this thought was resonating. Like the wonder of a child learning something new, she then said, "Just ask? It's that simple?" I smiled and said, "Yes. Just ask." So, she did ask, out loud, in her shower, and what poured out seeping into her heart was all the answers she has been working on receiving. She asked and then received, accepting the flowing grace of her open heart, her open faith; teaching her the ability to believe, to feel, to see all the gifts that make her this uniquely special person who was born whole. As she was receiving this knowledge, without fear she was returning to her original, perfect self. As the water ran off her body, so did her fears and doubts and these lessons of hurt that kept clouding her vision. These new gifts taught her wisdom to lift the veil of darkness. In the experience of holding on to harsh life lessons, she understood the meaning of these lessons and the impact of their residual energy. Accepting her gifts, fully allowing her awareness challenged her to experience rejuvenation, inviting new life. This new life, combined with her new gifts, gave her constructive tools for clearing and releasing toxins, washing them down the drain. She then was able to embrace her gifts of self-love, to forgive the ignorance and the damage of past experiences. She has risen from the damage and can respect it from afar while setting new, healthy boundaries. To say she is brand new is probably an accurate description. As her awareness expands, her Spiritual birth arises. The new soft essence around her face, depicts visual calm, strength, and kindness. She has developed, over time, the ability to peel back the layers, and she has learned in a short time the power of true forgiveness for herself and for the ignorance of another who may have inflicted pain upon her.

She knows, as I do, that pain and growth are the ingredients needed to be able to experience joy. A result of growing through this darkness, we know the pinpricks of light will show up, shine through, and lead the way. I encourage you now to ask - simply ask - then listen. You will be very surprised when you hear the calling from within, ego combined with Spirit, sharing your precious gifts with you.

Identifying your Spirit gifts and learning to put them into practice strengthens your gifts and leads you to receive added gifts. I encourage you to use your gifts, applying them to all you do in everyday living. Spiritual gifts will always be compatible with your worldly gifts. They seem to intertwine in a way that brings you peace, stability, and security, completing a state of true self. What to expect when you invite your Spiritual gifts within: A deeper awareness outside your personal world; wisdom; heightened intuition - hearing messages, seeing angelic signs. We all have these gifts. They are given to us from Divine Source that wants us to know, as well as experience, the gifts Source brings us. Take the time unwrap, digest, and accept your intuitive presents. They all are waiting for you to discover their magic.

BALANCE BETWEEN FLESH AND SPIRIT

I do not know about you, but I love being human! I love the way my body feels when I am eating a hot fudge sundae topped with whipped cream and sprinkled with salted peanuts. I love the way it tastes; in fact, I am confessing now: I am a foodie. Sometimes even a closet foodie. I love A&W Onion rings, McDonald's bacon and egg biscuit (in the United States). I love turkey dinner with all the trimmings, especially Joe's stuffing. I love pasta of every kind, and crab legs. I am a foodie and proud of it!

Being human allows me to grow my hair, to walk, to run, to ski, to climb, to dance and sing. It allows me to experience emotions that represent very big moments of joy and euphoria, and tears that represent a whole spectrum of feelings from love and happiness to sadness and grief. Being born human is like winning a Spiritual lottery; the chance to feel in the flesh what our Spirits cannot. Being human has taught me balance, fatigue, pain, love, peace, fear, compassion, and forgiveness.

There are times, however, now that I have had 25 years of healing lessons that I wish I could have made a difference to the people in my life by being a kinder, more responsible person. This wish is something I came here to write about. It is something I needed to reflect on and commit to standing up and addressing and releasing situations in my past, forgiving my ignorance and my actions. For many years, I was a mess: confused, conflicted, and completely lost. Being human is a gift we get to redeem, rediscover, and recommit to every second of our lives in these containers of flesh, blood, organs, and bone.

Being human reminds me today that the learning never stops; the lessons never quit. We are programmed to grow in this way. I truly believe, as I work with both worlds simultaneously, that our Spirit has all the time in the universe to be Spirit. Spirit is and has always been a constant, with a never-ending energy. Spirit is timeless. It is endless. It flows naturally, eternally, and is never in a hurry.

Our human body and our human flesh are different. Our human vessels, our bodies, are on the clock. We have only so many hours to live, to breathe, to experience and to learn. We all know this to be true. In my case, I still want the experience that being human gives me. I love human life and everything it offers, and I do not know if I will ever be ready to leave this world. There is so much diversity, so many things to discover, taste, feel, hold, identity, consider, desire, teach, and learn.

I have come to realize that I have experienced human form in more than one lifetime on this planet. I know this in my soul and in my mind, and this knowledge does not scare me at all. It intrigues me. I know by my continued desire for growth, that I have chosen many human lessons and lived the lives each one presented me and embraced the lessons they taught me. I also know some were harsh lessons of loss and death. I needed to experience these lessons to learn how to rise to light and love, and to identify what not to repeat.

I believe that Spirit energy, although a complete entity on its own, allows us our own Divine spark. I believe I have my own individual spark, unique to me, but also a part of the collective Spirit energy. I believe we are all this way: individuals, yet a part of the collective consciousness of Spirit energy. I believe we all get to choose and to be whom and what we need to be. I believe we get a say in what we need to learn and what we need to experience to grow.   Being human allows us to have those experiences.

When I am connected to my soul and ego essence, I learn love, kindness, consideration, and caring. Loving Spirit energy from Divine Source is a pure example of kindness. This source always knows what I need, but it is also wise enough to respect my human boundaries; enough, in fact, to ask before it delivers the truth I need to consider. Although loving Spirit is quick to send me signs to help me figure it out before my ego catches on, it also reminds me I am never alone in my quest for truth, education, and growth.

Divine Spirt has educated me in a deeper way by learning to respect its identity. Although it is not of ego (flesh), it originates from an intelligence, a wisdom that surpasses all time as we know it while we live in human form.   This energy provides us with an opportunity to experience diversified, tri-dimensional living; in body, mind, and Spirit, on this planet we call Earth. This planet and all human life breathe air. My belief is that body and Spirit together are the means of connection to the gift of the air I breathe, bringing me life. It is the first thing a newborn baby does: he or she fills their lungs with fresh air, bringing them life. The combination of the two elements connects us forever to both worlds: one of the flesh, and one of Divine Source.

Spirit graciously takes a back seat as we become human, and that relationship teaches us healthy boundaries imperative to developing an understanding of life here on this planet. Spirit never goes where it is not invited. If invited, it goes wherever you do, joining in and sharing your lessons and trials and tribulations. I think our ego always has a say in what we still need to learn. In Spirit, we study what we still need to accomplish and learn in human form; however, I believe our ego always has a say in what lessons we need to experience. I believe I get to choose, discuss, dissect, all I have come here to learn the many times I have traveled here. I know this to be my truth: that I have a chance, every, time to rise above any situation and learn new ways to love in a deeper wholeness. I believe that in being humbled and being human, flawed, scarred, I can heal from taking a good look at myself and others.   This information is invaluable to my growth, both in ego and in Spirit, teaching me necessary boundaries, allowing me to develop wisdom accumulated in the lessons.

I know that dark energy does not set healthy boundaries for me. I know the greed and speed of instant gratification takes methodical timing, giving me little chance to process the consequences. Dark energy gains its power through greed, lust, and human weakness. This energy has no heart, no soul, only negativity, darkness, and suppression of unresolved issues. This is how it traps you. It makes promises of grand power with little work required. This is an illusion. If something looks too easy or too promising, pay attention to the loving energy in your body, gently advising you to select a different option. Look and seek the truth within your essence. Dark energy has no respect for foundation, ethics, or any type of unity, especially boundaries. It wants only to gain power as quickly as possible, destroying everything in its way. It teaches us, however, to always know, we have the power to rise above and accept the pinpricks of light. This bright white light will always shine for you in every darkness you encounter. You can always choose the light. This source will support you and will never forsake you. This divinity belongs to you; it is a part of your essence. You come from this source that lives with you in every interaction and every lesson. Every breath you take in, this source takes that breath with you.

Boundaries are formed in this balance of flesh (body) and Spirit and they grow with you as you progress. These boundaries build you, define you, and share what you share, teach what you teach to our world, and the Spirit world we are joined with. Learn to love yourself in every decision you make. Continue to work in, and through, the new set of boundaries as you grow. You are creating and establishing a new, refined you, as you continue to accumulate new inspirational wisdom!

ENERGY REVELATIONS

Becoming exposed to the essence of dark energy is like receiving frost bite causing the loss of sensation can, be a bit unnerving to say the least. The way I describe my personal experience of dark energy as it weaves its essence in and out of the chapters of this book allows the energy to express its purpose and its reality.

Away in Mexico, I experienced face to face, heart to heart, soul to soul, the real fear the fear that I have come to understand is the core, the nucleus that is the essence of darkness, belonging to dark energy.

This darkness sets in the soles of every human life form and the nucleus is geared to fear. This fear feeds the source. It's as simple and as profound as that. Fear feeds dark damp cold energy. As I see it, felt it, in the darkness I was surrounded in all alone, it spoke to me and tried to paralyze me. Of course, my body reacted as any human would react, for me I was very uncomfortable in the silence of the darkness so to avoid it I would turn on lights, watch stimulated technology on my tablet or my phone. I did whatever I could the first two weeks alone avoiding sinking into the pit of darkness and fear. After I started writing however I too started to receive the pinpricks of light I talk about throughout this book. Not only was I starting to see the light I was starting to understand both energies without fear.

Dark energy can only exist if we feed it and what feeds it is fear. If anyone is biblical or has heard the story about an angel named Lucifer who wanted to take over the reign of heaven, then you have heard that the dark energy was cast out of the celestials and sent to reign on earth. This is where the dark energy has built up home base, on our beautiful planet earth reigning in Spirit, reaping fear based, carnage destruction, possessing the ego of man. We get to choose we get to learn through the information that is accessible to all of us. Because I was raised in a Christian rooted family and was raised with Christian faith this is where I tend to get my information and what sits as truth in my solar plexes. I don't write this way to turn anyone off or upset anyone who may be an atheist, or prognostic, who is reading it's just what makes sense to me as I gathered my facts and experience in writing this book.

As I began to stop the fear, and I was able to do this by hearing the light and feeling the support I was able to discern how the dark energy operates and feeds to gain control and power. It was like I was observing and was given the truth and the information watching it work and spread like spider webs over the entirely of mankind.

Dark energy has a pulsating centre in its core that is made of fear. This living energy has power to infect and attract you. This energy is very sneaky as it is privy to you and who you are, after all it is Spiritual energy with intellect. It leers you into its web by emotionally keeping you in bondage by attaching what and who, you love. This energy is not concerned with the nucleus of humans that are naïve enough to stay stagnant and do not want to make any effort to change. These humans choose their own free will to stay in a place of complacent and comfort addicted to greed and the subliminal noise of dark energy. The dark energy already has what it needs from these people that feed its growing power. This energy as I see it has spider webs that extend from the fear base of it and attach it to everyone and everything by infecting you with emotions such as instant gratification, both physically and emotionally. Dark energy feeds on addictions and bad habits that cause what I call emotional hangovers, leaving you craving more of what substance or addition you are addicted too. These addictions of course reign in your human existence. As I suggested this is how dark energy sinks its spiders clawing into your flesh distracting you from the white light white source you come from this is the only power dark energy has reign over. Your human body, and the way you choose to live and choose your lessons and the actions you decide upon. Other emotions that feed fear from dark energy are anger, frustration, doubt, jealousy, guilt, expectations, vulnerability, and self-saturated closed-minded thinking. I was able to see this energy for what it is and how it infects us and how after it infects us spreads. When you are complacently committed to the source, you have given it permission to habitat. This energy is greedy, wanting to possess white light commitment, dark energy is after all the light workers in the world that are committed to working for Divine white light Spirit. This dark energy knows full well how much power light workers have and are connected too. This energy will not stop until it grows as big as it possibly can, dark energy is invested to take everything over.

White light energy is consistently thoughtful, patient, understanding we need to have the lessons we are constantly aggressively learning. Most human beings including myself avoid pain and the infliction it causes. Pain hurts on every level it saturates within. I, like you, avoid the inflictions pain cause me. White light is the origin of the essence of where I came from. I was born into flesh as Tracey with the connection of energy attached to my physical form. I come from love that is my original beginning. When I was born into flesh, I took my first breath I was given life but also brought living loving Spiritual energy of origin into the breath I took in this human existence. I came from love so, therefore it's my birthright no matter how dark my lessons get in this existence I still have a choice to forgive myself, be forgiven, and return to the nurturing love I came into life with teaching me what I needed to experience this time.

White light energy's core is constructed by the nucleus of love. Love is the core of what the energy is constructed of. The elements that make up this energy base are all the emotions that take time to process. They are not often instantaneously achieved. Some take years to learn and still after learning and accepting these attributes, continue to grow and rise us to a different state of elevation Spiritually, understanding the concept and flow of the virtue itself. Some of the attributes or emotion attained or gained in practice and acceptance of white light energy are compassion, consideration, kindness, truth, stability, acceptance, non- judgment, and forgiveness. Divine white light must be earned and must be a direct acceptance internally before it can be authenticated externally.

What was fascinating to learn was the way I was able to tap into Divine white light and listen as well as witness the non-judgment from the source. I was able to take so many things less personally even if I were to witness someone being a victim to a certain situation. This white light energy is attached to us, so in layman's terms, it also experiences all the trauma, drama, infliction, and pain we all feel and go through in the action of the infliction. This energy is with us all the way and never ever leaves us not even for one moment. This energy commits to us through all the good and all the bad. This energy does not have a human ego, so it does not feel the emotions we do. However, because we are beloved and belong to Source, it feels our pain it feels and supports all we go through without judgment or reprimand. Quick to forgive us if we ask for it and quick to take away any of the scar tissue or dark energy that is saturated within our physical body tri dimensionally. What was very interesting for me during this time out was I was the one in control of how long I was going to keep my body hostage by holding on to lower frequency scar tissue and blockages. I was the one who could let go and let white light redirect my attitude and my gratitude.

We are light beings. We have the power to embellish and consume the light we came from getting rid of unwanted dark energy that sneaks in the cracks causing fear and chaos emotionally exhaustion and outbursts of irrational behavior. All fear based all about control, or lack of control that all accumulate combustible power. If you pull the power source from darkness and plug in the power source of light you will not linger in negativity, or want, or fear. The darkness within becomes saturated with light, darkness simply cannot exist where there is light.

As I have said I do not fear darkness nor do I fear what it represents, I am heart felt grateful for all the lessons the darkness has taught me. The years I was saturated by poor choices, that have led me to know the difference, had I not had the experience I would not have a choice. I do say thank you to the lessons I never wish to repeat, and I do in some ways respect the energy of darkness and the lower frequency. If we did not have this energy to remind us every day how to rise above it, we could not keep working on the betterment of communication with and for each other. Most importantly, we could not respect love and encompass the whole meaning behind the nucleus of white light Divine energy.

I encourage all of you to rise above what you ever thought you could, or what you ever dreamed capable of. I encourage you to stay grounded reach deep within and hear the needs of what will help you attain a healthy balance of whole existence. This is a dedicated practice and a choice but once you decide to work towards your birthright and accept this love and responsibility you will see miracles manifest internally. Be patient, please be patient. Most times getting to the level of enlightenment you are seeking takes time and growth takes a while before you see or feel the results of it. The more you grow the more prana you will receive to feed the growth you have established within your internal foundation.

Do not be afraid to ask for help from Spirit fed source. I do all the time from my Mother- in- Law Betty, Anita Craiger, and Dr. Wayne Dyer. These people guide me not in flesh but have transitioned to Spirit. Frankly, many Spiritual light workers join me in meditation when I am in a session virtually or physically. Asking for Divine help is so important to help you grow also to assure you that you are never alone. Asking also helps in keeping your ego in check. Remember helping others is never about you, it is all about them. Even though you may feel lonely. Angels are a gift from Divine and ask them all to join you and ask for specific signs and messages. I love working with the angels they love working with us.

You are a human and Spirit combination, you deserve to know what you need to learn and how to address the knowledge that sits in the middle of your heart teaching you truth confidence and internal peace. This is your birthright. How you find your way to it, is your own yellow brick road during experience, but, know you will and know you deserve what you find at the end of your own cross, and your own sacrifices. YOU ALWAYS GET TO CHOOSE!

Tracey L. Pagana

STAYING IN THE EYE OF THE STORM

Ten months have passed since I first encouraged my fingers to crack open my lap top computer on an attempt to write about *Coming Out of Darkness*. My year has taken me down some roads I did not expect, quite literally as you have read along with me through Mexico and my precious time there last year, but also around a few bends and turns I did not expect in my awakening growth and full-on truth.

I have learned more about myself this year than I ever anticipated. Some of these lessons left me curled up in a ball of pain, internal heart ache, stripping off bandage after bandage seeking the pin pricks of light saturated in the antibiotics of Spiritual truth. Some old relationships have served their reason, season, and time, as we hug goodbye and carry on in our independent journeys of whole self or not, enlightened, or not, in truth or not. I have come to understand in the deepest way these separations are not personal but are growth. What I have really come to understand as I share with you, is that it is none of my business to interfere in anyone's life unless I am asked my thoughts. This is where I have done the most independent work on my true whole self. I still slip up often; offering things out of passion and connection, practice makes perfect, especially on this subject matter.

Initiating this thought and awareness has taught me that to come out of darkness fully stepping into the light, especially during one of the most challenging years our planet has witnessed cohesively in my entire lifespan. It has heightened my awareness in the gift of quiet prayer and perspective, taught me a whole new way of communication and consideration towards mankind in general. This year has forced hundreds and thousands of people the gift of slowing down, reconnecting, authentic communication, going back to simple basic tools of delivering common sense practices, and community support. This year has brought so many shock waves of instability and has made us all question equality, boundaries, community service, and kindness.

I choose, above all, to stay positive. I choose, above all, to have an even more intimate relationship to my Divine source. I choose every day to practice habitual, ritual and Spiritual habits knowing in me and for me, they make a huge difference to my energy. I can then consciously stay connected to the whole world infecting others with beautiful white light. Energy is contagious, it spreads like a wild bush fire. This means dark energy can do the same but has an entirely negative not positive effect on wherever it spreads.

My journey through the first two months of last year was the beginning of me fully recognizing what an awakening feels like after you cut all the cords away that were freezing you in fear. It was the start of a thawing out of my entire being as the white light cut cords of fear within me to help me feel the warmth that was there underneath the layers of my life all along. The fear was clogging my entire being in a blanket of untruth and sabotaging me in a way by trying to keep me in a frozen state so I would not slip away from the dark clutches that had me in the place of submission. This darkness wanted to feed off me and would have continued had I not found the tools I needed in my awareness to cut them away.

I want to share this as I feel its super important at this point in this book. Because life has changed so much this year, for so many of us, we have had to find other ways to communicate, expand our old way of thinking and getting creative. This is also very true for people working, facilitating, and channeling messages from Divine, while also teaching others how to discover their own healing energy. I would have never imagined my virtual sessions would be so accessible in the way one on one has always been. But Spirit work is energy, so I find that virtual sessions are extremely potent and just as effective as in person one on one sessions. Why would they not be? Divine source is everywhere.

I was delivering a recorded session for a client the other day and have come to do an impromptu meditation at the end of a message delivered to the client. In the meditation I distinctly heard this message from source.

When you unplug from what feeds you!
You can reconnect to what needs you!

Staying in the eye of the storm is your safest, wisest, harbour. The eye is calm, and you can see the darkness and the light at the same time at any angle. You can stay warm, wise, and competent. You have both clarity and equilibrium. You are not surprised or shocked, as you have the whole vision. You have the wisdom you need to feel, hear, see, from Divine source, guides, angels, and loved ones who are in Spirit form come and support you as they sit with you in the eye. I have come to understand I need to be more grey than black and white as I navigate others reaching for their hands, hearts, leading them out of their own storm to a safe soft quiet reflection. We all have a job to do. Some will only go so far and quit because it may change too many things that they have grown accustomed to in their life this time around. Some will settle, put a smile on their lips that does not match the smile in their heart and soul, which is ok, as it is their choice to live or exist in this life the best way, they choose to navigate it. The freedom for me is to love and accept the choices people make. Remember always, that you do not have to agree or even like the choice others choose, however, I deeply encourage you to love at all cost. Trust me when I say it will absolutely be in your very best interest of the highest good to your highest self.

Tracey L. Pagana

As my internal tapestry weaves its rich mahogany and burgundy, greens, and purple hues of lush living Spirit connected energy, new soil, has been laid, providing a new foundation. It has been born, as I shed layers and layers of old scar tissue and fear. Accepting my entirety deeply embedded in my solar plexes. It has a new core structure teaching me through my experience and travel and meeting of genuine Spirit filled simple humbled people from all walks of life the power of quiet power and action.

I encourage you all to take a step out, explore something you never thought you ever would. Make a personal connection with your internal birth right, your healer within. Get to know all parts of you; the good, the bad, the ugly, the broken, and the beautiful. Accept it all and hug yourself often. Slow down and do a slow dance with the power of quiet silence. Let your internal soul essence take the lead for a while. Step out of your comfort zone and try something new that might make you feel uncomfortable even vulnerable and learn the experience of your deepest most honesty.

I encourage you all to take a deep dive and find your whole entire self. If you find yourself in a place of darkness, take out your survival kit, light a match and allow Divine source to send a hand, an angel, a loved one or a guide to take your hand and lead you out of your own darkness. Coming out of darkness you will discover the light was there inside you all along. You just had to stop and slow down enough to discover the treasure you already had. Is it hard? I am not going to lie at this point. It would not do any good to lie to you as it is going to be one of the hardest journeys you ever take. But ask me if it's worth it or anyone else who has said yes to full on self-truth, accountability, and acceptance. There is no other way to exist. The gifts never stop arriving at the door of your heart.

Resources

BEYOND BELIEF

I want to introduce you to one of my soul friends, Holly McGeorge, and I dedicate this chapter to her. I have an entirely different version of our Divinely orchestrated connection than Holly has, and I am sure when she takes the time to write her autobiography, Holly will choose to write differently about how our paths crossed. Here is my version.

Holly is a psychic medium who lives in West Lorne, Ontario, Canada. I first heard Holly's name mentioned, possibly by one of my clients, and her name landed on my heart with a thud. Before meeting Holly, I had only ever experienced four or five readings by psychics in my entire life. I had no interest in going to someone who had these gifts on a regular basis, but in saying that, I have much respect for authentic, gifted psychics. As I said, her name landed on my heart with a thud, and I knew it had been planted there by Spirit in a way that was rather disturbing for me.

Over the next few weeks, I would have repeated thoughts that I needed to call and check on her. It was annoying! I caught myself wondering what could I possibly offer her, and why was I getting these messages to contact her? I felt deeply that these messages were more about Holly's needs than mine, and it was causing me grave concern. It felt like a constant voice from Spirit, suggesting strongly that I reach out to Holly.

The voices inside my head, my heart, and my gut kept urging me to call her, so one day that is what I did. Anyone who knows me - yes, I see you smiling - knows that when I am called to something, I usually spout it all out in one huge big breath, covering a lot of ground, voicing my thoughts with many words. I can say for certain I am passionate, so much so that, at times, I am like a dog with a bone, especially when I have a message for someone from Spirit. This message to Holly was from Spirit.

I remember our first, somewhat awkward first call. I am sure she thought I was a crackpot, or better yet, a stalker! I called her a few times before I think she felt

112

comfortable with our conversation. I remember telling her she needed to protect herself more, and I wanted to not only send her my books, but also a large Shiva Lingam for grounding. The Shiva is my very favorite ancient healing stone of all time. I knew without a shadow of a doubt she desperately needed that stone in her presence as she continued to do her work. The books and stone arrived on May 30, 2018. Holly and I have been growing together for almost two years now. If I am being honest, sometimes I think we have been connected far longer than those two years.

I also remember, early on in our connection, feeling a very strong need to call Holly and asking her to take off her socks and sit in the pond on her property. Holly remembers the call, noting that she was certain she had never mentioned having a pond. She complied with my request and went to the pond, rolled up her pant legs, and stuck her feet in the water, and she was able to release stress that had been building for some time. I was able to talk her through releasing that stress into the healing water of her pond.

On another occasion, I could feel that she was deeply stressed and sad, and I called her. At first, she was reluctant to share what was troubling her, but then she confessed she had been on her knees cleaning and had burst into tears about a personal struggle she was caught up in. I felt so blessed that I was able to help her talk it through. I knew for sure we were sent to each other from our Spirit Father and her beloved mom, and our relationship provided both of us with a safe place of shared soul connection to sort out, collaborate, and discuss all things sacred and personal to both of us.

What cemented this relationship for me another phone conversation about our healing work and the incredible responsibility that comes with it. I was driving at the time, talking hands-free, of course, and the conversation was so intense for both of us that I pulled over to finish our conversation. It was in that moment I understood our unique gifts, combined, would continue to help anyone seeking their own gifts. I knew in that moment that both our lives would change and that we had come into each other's lives to learn the true meaning of trust, through a gift given to both of us by the unconditional loving energy we both originate from.

To say my life has changed since meeting Holly would be a huge understatement. I loved my healing work, working for Father Spirit and white light energy and angels and guides. But I loved it in my own time, overseeing my destiny and how many clients I felt I could handle at one time. I loved my simple, quiet life and the order I felt comfortable with, and my ability to set tight boundaries around my safe place. I had a quieter life before I met Holly, but I was limiting my potential and trying to control the outcome.

Holly has her own unique story to tell, and I believe she will one day share her story, her life, her love for Spirit and all living beings. She has had a very tough life with many lessons, suffering pain to a degree that has broken her body, her heart, and her Spirit more than once. She kept getting back up, brushing it off, moving forward. She has overcome many obstacles in her life and has made huge personal sacrifices time and time again. I have, over the past two years, been witness to her tireless devotion to her clients and her long hours of work. I have witnessed her extended efforts to counsel anyone who needs assistance from this powerhouse. I have had the privilege and the honour of working with her side by side, as well as supporting each other in live videos, respecting each other as we exchange Spiritual gifts with and through each other for the greater cause of healing and peace.

We have become workmates and playmates, sharing, and trusting and even forgiving each other. This journey sharing and living life with Holly has been a journey of healing. Light workers can find themselves congested, exhausted, and depleted over time. Our work is long and can be physically and emotionally taxing, intense, and private, as we vow in our authenticity to never divulge what does not belong to us. For me, having a light worker partner like Holly saves me. Without guilt or divulging of information that does not belong to us, we can support each other in our work. Holly's sense of humor, her grace, her respect, and her foundation of truth, topped off with a deep and fresh honesty, make me feel I am never alone working for Spirit. I have a human partner who relates to the same emotional pledge we both accepted and signed up for when we joined our Spiritual team of white light energy workers. Our lives seem to be entwined, and we are both committed to the work we love.

In 2019, Holly took me with her to California to introduce me to some of her beautiful clients she had established there over time. One client had worked previously with Holly and had invited Holly and her husband to stay with them for a vacation in 2018. Anyone who knows our Holly would not be surprised to hear she inevitably turned her vacation time into work. I understand, as these gifts we work with do not have a shut-off valve, and when she hears messages she acts. Their visit in 2018 went so well that Holly was asked to return in 2019, and I was extremely fortunate to be asked to go along to work with her. This earth angel, our host, kindly extended an invitation for me to stay with them. As well, working and supporting our host's personal circle of friends, as well as inviting strangers she had not yet met into her home for eleven days of healing. What an example of pure faith and trust! These beautiful people exposed their private space and hearts, showing the world not only who they are but also the action of pure love. They knew deeply that something was happening that was bigger than any of us could explain. It was a very powerful time of body/soul connection, with all of us experiencing deep, personal growth.

Our hosts, Beth and Keith opened their hearts and their home to us. They shared their personal space for us to work in, fed us delicious homemade meals, and made us feel like we belonged. How does that happen? How grateful we were and how blessed a life Holly and I share! It is a gift we get to experience. I know that Holly is destined to experience great things, as she does not belong to just me; she belongs to all the people who fall in love with this genuine gemstone. I am lucky to have had the opportunities she has been kind enough to share with me. I have promised her that my answer will always be yes. if she has an idea or wants me to see one of her clients, it will be yes. I will always support where she grows and will never be far if she needs or wants to reach out. She knows, I know, we were given to each other by Spirit, and our connection is both personal and Spiritual.

Together, Holly and I commit to this loving, healing energy; although, some days for Holly are almost humanly impossible. As she rises from her sleep with few hours of rest, her body is racked with pain so intense it takes two cups of coffee for her body to wake up and recover enough to function properly. Still, she just keeps on rising out of her own darkness. Her intent is for others as she helps them to discover they, too, are born whole. Holly attempts to shed light, helping all to embrace their own essence through the validation of truth and messages she receives from the Spirits of loved ones confirming they are still around. This allows us all to believe we can rise and find our own way out of darkness to embrace life.

Holly McGeorge: holly_mcgeorge@yahoo.ca

GHOST AND ENERGY CLEARING

I would like to introduce you to two gifted healers in ghost and energy clearing. My recollection, when first hearing about Tanya and Dave Steele, was around six years ago. One of my soul friends, Natasha, was having a hard time clearing some energy from her home, which led her to finding Dave and Tanya. As Natasha began to share her experience with me, explaining what Dave and Tanya had done and how it had helped her, I somehow felt that I would also need their services one day.

In Tanya's words, "It is difficult to describe what we do, and many people cannot wrap their heads around it. We get rid of negative energies, which comprise a whole host of categories, resulting in healing for our clients. We remove negative entities and energies from people, places, animal companions, and objects. We use and connect with the gift of psychic, intuitive, healing energy that works in our own lives, as well as in the lives of our clients."

About six months after Natasha shared her experience with me, I received a rather upsetting call from a woman who needed assistance I knew I could not provide. She talked to me in the most desperate voice. She was beyond scared! I remember the phone call like it was yesterday. I was on my lunch break, standing in a little grassy area my company had designed for its employees to read or eat lunch. I was in the gazebo when my phone rang. The woman's voice was frantic. She and her husband had inherited property in Scotland and had just recently returned from staying in the home. His relative, an uncle, had left the property to them. He was an angry man, his Spirit restless, and he did not like her. He tried to hurt her physically, his Spirit even once grabbing her in the bathtub, trying to drown her. She was in total distress on the call. I honestly knew I did not have the tools to even try and address this issue with her. I did, however, teach her how to release what she could not control. I directed her and her husband to please ask for protection and to go outside and stand in barefoot in the grass, releasing energy that did not belong to them into Mother Earth. Then, I gave her Dave's and Tanya's number and insisted she hire them.

She did contact them, and she called me after they did their work, expressing her joy in the release of the energy haunting their home that was taken out and sent to the light. Tanya and Dave are the real deal, and I love and respect them for the courageous work they do every day, bringing light into very dark places. This same woman came to me for a healing session and found peace and joy and new birth in her session of personal healing. She had had to address the other situation before she could ever find a personal healing within herself.

Teamwork! Where would we be without a team of loving, trusting, compatible light workers? My personal experience with this couple's energy work went deeper than I even realized. Not only did they clear my Joe and me of energy that was sticking to us, but they continue to work with us, releasing and re-releasing in clearings. They continue, on a regular basis, working hard at clearing me so that I can continue to do the work I do. After a clearing with Dave and Tanya, they send you a detailed report in writing that explains what they did, what was being cleared, and the reasons for this clearing. I can personally confirm that their reporting of any lower frequency energies is authentic and accurate. I have felt the effects of this energy being cleared and have become aware of the healings in my personal relationships. The energy work these two provide gives me a chance to recover, as well as discover, a true sense of inner peace, with less chatter from the lower frequencies that can hide out inside my body. Spreading this light in these dark places keeps me healthy and focussed on my gifts and the work that Father Spirit keeps calling me deeper into.

Tanya, Dave and I collaborate often, and in the honest relationship we share, we have created a bond that is stronger than I can explain. It is a Trinity of love and soul strength, providing us a place for discussion and deep sharing of our gifts, knowing we all have unique gifts to offer through and for each other.

I have referred clients who I know require a session with them before I can help them heal, and, at times, turn down clients so they can go through the proper channels of healing before they come to me. I know they need to address the darkness that is interfering with and constricting their light, their path. As I have discussed, lower frequency energies can sneak into open portals, saturating and infecting our bodies, hearts, minds, and souls.

These two magicians, I often refer to Tanya as a wise witch and Dave a wise wizard, have a purpose and a mission to stamp out, drag out, and dismiss these unwanted energies that take up space wherever they can find an opening. They work tirelessly, diligently, often sending 11-to-15-hour day long healings out to clients. They have worked for years developing a formula and a process that work in dealing with the lower frequencies of darkness that live in our environment.

Dave and Tanya email: Tanyalight19@live.com   Dave13@icloud.com

THE DAINTY DRAGON

Lisa Wright is a very, talented, artist who has a unique gift as she works creating beautiful magic living crystal creations. She makes a variety of creative expression in her own unique technique. I call her my fairy angel. She is soft spoken, kind, authentic and gentle. She has so much power in her quiet presence you might not even know she was there she is so soft spoken. But her power is undeniable.

I have personally come to love crystals in a way that has surprised me, supported my practice, and just comforts me. Lisa has provided me with her huge loving generous heart, many tools to help people heal deeper in a session. Lisa had a dream and after her dream created from the dream a tool I use regularly in session is a long chakra alignment crystal cord collectively connecting all the colours that coordinate with the chakras on your body that align perfectly when you lay it on the client. It helps to clear out also aids in cleansing and unblocking a chakra that may be blocked. I love the one she made for me to use with clients, after I use the tool in a session, I can clean it and clear ready to use again. She makes two different styles.

I received a precious gift of Moldavite from a very beautiful person his name is George (it's a tektite (glass) formed from a meteorite that impacted the earth about 15 million years ago) it's quite rare and extremely powerful. I knew it needed something really, special to house it. I commissioned her to take it and make me something I could wear while in sessions with my clients. She came to my home took the crystal and did research on the glass itself and then she added all the authentic gems stones that would enhance its energy to the highest vibrations. It was so powerful when I got it back from Lisa that I had to wear it at first for just a short time as the crystals were introducing me to its full potential power. I wear it in every session.

Lisa kindly often offers me bracelets and other crystal beauties she has created to pass on to clients who need a little extra love and guidance. Lisa is very giving of her gifts and shares a great love for the crystal babies she has come to know as mother earth treasures.

Lisa can be hired and commissioned one on one, or virtual for personal necklaces, bracelets, for specific, beautiful, everyday wear and protection. Her creativity never stops she is known designing wire fairy art. Fairies with wire wings and pieces of Mother Nature crystals embedded in them. Very, unique, with the added element of healing energy.

Lisa email: lisk_2@hotmail.ca

TOOLS I USE DAILY

Human Pendulum: Get your body to stand in a very, comfortable position. If you are a little anxious shake your body out and take a few deep breaths. Close your eyes stand still in the moment find a quiet place to ask yourself two questions. First, ask a question you know is a yes answer. Wait for your body to move it will and when it does it will make a full motion movement. This is your yes. Ask yourself another yes question to confirm the movement. Do the same with a question with a no answer and wait for your body to move. It will also make a complete full motion movement. Ask another no question to confirm the movement. This is your soul's way of helping you out in a situation that you may need clarity and guidance on, that overrides your ego if you are in a state of exhaustion or stress or anxiety. I have come to rely on this powerful tool often in my life. I also love sharing it clients to help them on their journey to heal and wholeness.

Prayer: Prayer for me has become even more personal than ever before. I find prayer more like a conversation that I would have with a best friend, or a dad, that lives inside the very core of my heart. Prayer has become a personal dialogue of banter and communication on something that is tenable for me not above me or separated from me but kind and soft loving and caring. I am alone often, but never lonely, because I feel like the whole universe, who I always have with me, somehow lets me know it is with me. If we could only see what walks beside us in Spirit and supports us with immense love and protection, we would truly never fear anything again. So, find your own prayer, find your own unique personal way to connect to the source you come from, and the source will never disconnect from you.

Protection: Ask for protection often. Ask for all the angels to stand by your side, call on them by name, research them, read about them, educated yourself on what they do and how they work and what gifts they bring to share with us. Ask your own soul what your gifts are and take time to see the signs that manifest to teach you, whether it be in nature or in numbers in licence plates. Seek and you will discover your own specific tools in your own unique toolbox. Use your words wisely they can be your most powerful tool you own.

Be well, stay blessed, stay wise, stay whole, and create your own unique authenticity it is your birthright and your own personal destiny. There is room for everyone to grow in this world. May peace reign in your hearts as you grow infecting your own world with your own luminous light!

www.ingramcontent.com/pod-product-compliance
Lightning Source LLC
Chambersburg PA
CBHW072145090426
42739CB00013B/3289

* 9 7 8 0 5 7 8 8 4 0 2 4 6 *